D0396365

Baby Belson

"More English than the English"

A Very Social History of Victoria

by

Terry Reksten

Orca Book Publishers, Victoria, B.C., Canada

Copyright © 1986 by Terry Reksten

Canadian Cataloguing in Publication Data

Reksten, Terry, 1942 -
  More English than the English

  Includes index.
  Bibliography: p. 192
  ISBN 0-920501-03-6

  1. Victoria (B.C.) — History. 2. Victoria
(B.C.) — Social conditions. I. Title.
FC3846.4.R44 1986   971.11'34   C86-091231-0
F1089.5.V6R44 1986

Published with the assistance of the
British Columbia Heritage Trust.

Orca Book Publishers
3824 Cadboro Bay Rd.
Victoria, B.C.
Canada, V8P 5E6

Typeset by AMS Graphics Shop, University of Victoria.
Printed by D.W. Friesen and Sons Ltd., Altona, Manitoba.

For Don

Victoria, c. 1889

Contents

FOREWORD

"More English Than The English" is not a formal, comprehensive history of Victoria. Instead it is selective and anecdotal and is intended to provide a sense of the developing city and a feeling for the times.

Written for those who might not usually find pleasure in reading about the past, it is not a reference book. However, it contains little-known facts and introduces some forgotten characters — enough to interest, and perhaps surprise, those who count themselves history "buffs."

History seems to come alive when one can locate physical evidence of the past. Throughout the text, the reader will find keys to sixty-one historical sites or points-of-interest. Beginning on page 156 these sites are listed and are briefly described and maps are included to aid in their location.

The sites are cross-referenced with the text so that the reader who is in the city for a short time might consult the maps, discover which sites are within an evening's stroll or drive and read that part of the text which relates to those particular locations before setting off to explore.

Notes on sources have been kept to a minimum, but have been carefully chosen to properly acknowledge indebtedness and to serve as a guide to those who might want to further explore any particular topic.

Many people have helped in the preparation of this book. Since 1980 I have been teaching *Victoria; A "Lady" with a Past*, a local history offered by Camosun College and this book reflects the enthusiasms and the suggestions of all those who have joined me in that class. Always helpful were Ian Baird of the University of Victoria library and many staff members at the Victoria City Archives and the Provincial Archives. Special thanks are due to Ron Buchanan, Bruce Gibson-Bean, Michael Halleran, George Radford, Martin Segger, Stuart Stark, Michael Wale, Bobby Weir and Candy Wyatt for sharing their research, their advice and their expertise.

I am grateful to Don and Jane and Norah for patiently accepting a house littered with papers, files and photographs as the project grew to take over every room and who didn't ask, "When will you be finished?" more than a dozen times. And I would like to thank my aunt, Margaret Hartt, for all the times she thought about phoning and didn't.

This book would not have been started if Bob Tyrrell had not come up with the idea and would not have been completed without his encouragement. Thanks Bob.

INTRODUCTION

"More English than the English" was a phrase Emily Carr used to describe her father. And it was true enough of Richard Carr and other English-born Victorians who sought to create a society based on a nostalgic, half-remembered or imagined England. But in many ways the phrase is misleading, suggesting that Victoria was *like* England, that it was and is "a little bit of old England." And of course it isn't and it never was. Instead it was "San Francisco on The Solent," a unique combination of English social values and American architecture with a population which included English, Blacks, Chinese, Scots, Irish, Germans, Indians and Americans.

"Father wanted his place to look exactly like England," Emily remembered. "He planted cowslips and primroses and hawthorn hedges and all the Englishy flowers." But while he might have wanted it to look like England, he didn't want it to *be* England. After making a modest fortune in California, he had returned "home," but he had been twenty-four years away and he was soon disillusioned. "I used to think there was nothing like England, and the English," he confided to his diary, "but now I find they are not exactly what I thought they were." Within a year he had decided to return to North America. He deliberately chose a British colony rather than an American state, but he would have been disappointed if he had discovered that Victoria resembled England too closely. What he hoped to find was a town in which British traditions were combined with American progressiveness, a city that represented the best of both worlds.

I. Fort Victoria

1.
"Here Before Christ"

Any history of Victoria must begin with the Hudson's Bay Company. The city grew around Fort Victoria, built by the company in 1843. HBC fur trader James Douglas served as Governor of the Colony of Vancouver Island and retired Company employees were members of the general assembly. The HBC's hold on the Fur Trade Reserve, several thousand acres of land closest to the fort, allowed them to dictate settlement patterns. Indeed, men of the Hudson's Bay Company exerted so strong an influence over the town during its formative years that Victorians grumbled that they acted as if HBC stood for "Here Before Christ."[1]

Founded in 1670 as the *Company of Adventurers of England Trading into Hudson's Bay*, the HBC had, by the beginning of the nineteenth century, expanded its field of operation across the continent. For a time Fort Vancouver, built on the Columbia River during the 1820's, had served as the Company's western headquarters. Furs, collected at Fort St. James on Stuart Lake, at Fort George at the junction of the Nechako and Fraser Rivers and at other Company outposts scattered throughout New Caledonia and the Columbia District, were carried on horseback and by canoe down to Fort Vancouver where they were loaded aboard an HBC ship for transport to London.

FORT VANCOUVER, 1845. *Built in 1824 on the banks of the Columbia River, Fort Vancouver served as the Pacific headquarters of the Hudson's Bay Company until 1847 when Fort Victoria assumed that role.*

2

While the governments in London and Washington negotiated the location of the boundary line between British and American territories, fur traders from both countries shared the trade of the Columbia District. Once the boundary issue was settled both American and British traders would find it easy to operate only on their own side of the line. The HBC, suspecting that the line might follow the Columbia, had carefully sited Fort Vancouver on the river's north bank where their establishment would be on the British side of the boundary. But by 1842 it was becoming increasingly apparent that the 49th parallel rather than the Columbia would become the agreed-upon demarcation line. As a precaution against that eventuality, the London-based company decided that it might be prudent to explore the southern tip of Vancouver Island, which they were sure would remain in British hands, to seek out a favourable site for the construction of an establishment that could, if necessary, assume the functions of Fort Vancouver. Given this assignment was James Douglas, the thirty-nine year old fur trader who would come to be intimately connected with the development of Victoria and who would become known as the Father of British Columbia.

James Douglas was born out of wedlock in 1803 in Demerara, British Guiana. His father was John Douglas, a Glasgow-based merchant who spent some years in Demerara managing a sugar plantation. His mother was Barbados-born Martha Ritchie, the daughter of a "free coloured woman."[2] When John Douglas returned to Scotland he left Martha and her children behind. But even though he married and began a second family, he retained an interest in his Guianese children and in 1812 James and his brother were brought to Scotland to complete their education.

In 1819 when he was sixteen, James Douglas joined the fur trade. Sent to New Caledonia in 1825, he served as a clerk under trader William Connolly at Fort St. James. It was while he was at Fort St. James that an incident occurred that might well have ended his career.

Connolly was away and twenty-five year old Douglas had been left in charge of the fort when he learned that an Indian who was suspected of having murdered a trader five years earlier had returned to the area and was encamped with the Carrier Indians at Stuart Lake. Douglas and a small party of men from the fort marched into the Indian village, where the culprit was found cowering under a blanket. According to Indian witnesses, Douglas ordered the man clubbed to death. When the body resembled a mass of "shapeless jelly," Douglas directed that a rope be tied around its neck. The corpse was then dragged back to the fort where it was fed to the fort's dogs.[3] Throughout his life, Douglas would deny this version of events. The man, he would claim, had been taken into custody and "executed later."[4] But as HBC Governor George Simpson observed, Douglas was capable of becoming "furiously violent when roused" and to the Indians at Stuart Lake, Douglas became an enemy rather than a partner in a mutually beneficial trading enterprise.

Vastly outnumbered and at all times vulnerable to attack, the men of the HBC depended on Indian good will for their survival. And that good will would continue only so long as the natives considered themselves to have been treated fairly. Judging Douglas to be all but useless at Fort St. James,

3

the Company transferred him to Fort Vancouver where he was assigned to work as an accountant.

JAMES DOUGLAS. *There was "something grand and majestic" about James Douglas. Tall, muscular and broad shouldered, Douglas was an imposing figure in spite of the poor fit of his London-ordered clothes.*

When he left Fort St. James in January of 1830, Douglas was accompanied by Amelia, the daughter of William Connolly and his Cree Indian wife Suzanne. In 1828 when sixteen year old Amelia married Douglas "by the custom of the country" she had entered into a form of marriage considered to be non-binding by many fur traders who regarded their Indian or half-breed wives as only temporary companions. When he was transferred to another post, the trader simply left his current cohabitant behind to take her chances with the man who succeeded him. Amelia was more fortunate, for in 1837 when the opportunity presented itself Douglas re-married her before an Anglican clergyman.

Amelia, who had been Douglas' wife for nine years before they were married, may have insisted that he regularize their union for by then she had witnessed her father's repudiation of her mother, Suzanne. William Connolly had 'married' Suzanne in 1803. For almost thirty years Suzanne had lived with him, bearing his children and accompanying him wherever he was sent by the Company. In 1831 Connolly retired from the HBC and taking Suzanne with him, he moved to Montreal. The following year, however, Connolly decided to marry a cousin, Julia Woolrich, an "amiable and accomplished" white woman. His relationship with Suzanne being an impediment to that union, he claimed that no legal marriage had ever existed between them. Suzanne slipped back to the north-west where she died in a convent in 1862. It was not until five years after her death that the Supreme Court, called upon to determine Connolly's legal heirs, deemed her marriage to have been valid.[5]

But if Amelia did not share her mother's fate, her life was affected by misfortunes of a different kind. When she stood before the Reverend Beaver to be married at Fort Vancouver in 1837, Amelia had already borne James six children and buried all but one of them. Between 1829 and 1854 Amelia gave birth to thirteen children. Only four of them survived her.

AMELIA DOUGLAS. *An energetic, bustling, capable woman, Amelia Douglas was known for her shyness, her kindness and the "sharpness" with which she raised her children.*

Douglas, as he sailed around the southern tip of Vancouver Island in 1842, studied several sites, any of which might have become the location of the future city of Victoria had Douglas selected it.[6] The deep protected inlet at Sooke was promising except for the high, steep, rocky shoreline and the strong current that ran through the inlet's entrance with the change of tides. Metchosin was a "very pretty place" with a supply of fresh water but the anchorage was exposed and would be insecure in rough weather. At Esquimalt Douglas found "one of the best harbours on the coast," but otherwise, he concluded, it possessed no attraction.

The site Douglas called Camosack seemed ideal. As a harbour, it was no better than some of the others he had inspected, but where those anchorages were surrounded by rocks and forests, at Camosack there was clear land within fifty yards of the shoreline on which the fort could be built and nearby he discovered a "range of plains nearly six miles square containing a great extent of valuable tillage and pasture land."

The Company accepted Douglas' recommendation and in March of 1843, he returned to Camosack to select the precise location of the fort. At first, he confided to his journal, he was "at a loss where to place the Fort." But after mulling the problem over, he chose a spot where a section of steep, rocky shoreline formed a natural wharf where ships could lie with their sides grazing the rocks. (*site 15*)

Within a quadrangle, 300 by 330 feet, the fort would be constructed according to standard HBC plans. Cedar logs some twenty-two feet long were driven four feet into the ground to form a palisade or stockade. An octagonal two-storied bastion, built of heavy squared logs, loopholed for musketry and provided with eight cannon bays was built at the south-east corner of the palisade. Once the work was underway, Douglas sailed for Fort Vancouver leaving the construction of the fort under the supervision of Charles Ross.

2.
"the very Elysium of Company posts"

Poor Charles Ross! If he was not born with a melancholy spirit, he soon developed one in the service of the Hudson's Bay Company. Like most other Company officers, Ross was a Scot. Born in Inverness and a contemporary of James Douglas, he joined the company in 1818. He served in Eastern Canada under the watchful eyes of experienced Chief Traders, men who were usually capable of recognizing in their clerks those frames of mind that might render them unable to deal with isolation and loneliness. But Ross' potential for sinking into depression must have escaped their detection for in 1824 he was transferred to a Company post west of the Rockies in the wilds of New Caledonia.

Ross was not the only trader to find New Caledonia a "land of sin and misery" but unlike men such as James Douglas, John Tod and Dr. William Fraser Tolmie, Ross lacked that "firmness of mind" that stiffened a man's resolve to remain intellectually alert and mentally active during the many months he spent without European companionship.

Wherever he was moved by the Company, James Douglas lugged along a 45-volume set of English classics. John Tod became an inveterate letter writer, his correspondence developing into a vehicle not only for conveying snippets of gossip to and about his fellow traders but also for debating engrossing problems such as the existence of God and the possibilities of life after death. Dr. William Fraser Tolmie, who combined medical duties with those of a fur trader, became absorbed in his avocation of botany and spent much of his time in the woods where he happily searched for specimens of native flora.

But Ross was cut from a different cloth. Content to fill his mind with the echoes of past conversations, Ross found his life in the Company's service one of "dreary solitude."[7]

The trader had little work to occupy his mind, Ross complained. But even so it was noted by the Company that in the year or two after Ross was sent to command a fur-trading post, trade at that post declined.

In 1841, after HBC Governor George Simpson sent him a list of words and phrases to be translated into the language of the Bella Bella and Bella Coola Indians, Ross was forced to admit that, in spite of the fact that he had been trading with them for four years, his knowledge of their language was "very limited."

Ross seems to have enjoyed neither writing nor receiving letters. When in the spring of 1843 a letter from his sister Eppy finally reached him, Ross replied that he had avoided writing to her for the last ten years because he was afraid that his letter might be answered by the news that she was dead.

As Ross put it with his characteristic cheerfulness and tact, "I preferred to remain in blissful ignorance . . . rather than run the risk of being told that ruthless fate had left me alone of my father's house."

In 1822 Ross had married, 'by the custom of the country', Isabella, a half-breed woman he had met at Lac La Pluie. And he had taken Isabella and their growing family with him wherever he was posted. But while James Douglas might view his wife and family as the "tender ties" that bound him to the west, Ross regarded his wife and nine children with resignation rather than affection.

"She is not . . . exactly fitted to sit at the head of a nobleman's table," he described Isabella. "She is a native of the country, and as to beauty quite as comely as her husband."

His children were a worry rather than a comfort. "My chief regret is their growing wild around me," he wrote from Fort McLoughlin. "The whole are with me here, nor do I see the least possibility of respectably disposing of any of them so long as we remain in this unchristian wild."

When HBC Governor George Simpson visited Charles Ross at Fort McLoughlin, he found him in a "nervous state."

"Than our way of life in this dreary wilderness nothing can be more dark and insipid," Ross stated, and Simpson, admitting that he was "exceeding

VANCOUVER ISLAND.—THE HUDSON BAY COMPANY'S ESTABLISHMENT.

FORT VICTORIA. *Construction of Fort Victoria began in 1843. When this illustration appeared in the* Illustrated London News, *August 26, 1848, the fort remained the only European settlement on Vancouver Island.*

anxious" about Ross' state of mind, decided that in the interests of preserving his sanity he should be transferred to the "very Elysium" of Company posts, Fort Victoria.

"The sudden transition from the comparative seclusion of Fort McLoughlin to the stirring scenes of this place, has been sufficiently trying to myself. In fact I never before was in such a turmoil in my life. For what with Building — fortifying — Shipping — farming — Indians etc. there is quite enough for me to do."

After Fort McLoughlin which Ross said enjoyed "almost constant rains two-thirds of the year," the weather at Fort Victoria was certainly an improvement. From June to November, they experienced nothing but bright, sunny days.

"The climate is perhaps *too fine*," Ross reported.

By January of 1844 as the winter closed in, Ross' thoughts turned inward. He was bothered by an old complaint, which he described as "coldness & an irregularity of the Bowels."

"Pray can you do anything for me?" he asked Dr. Tolmie. The doctor's usual prescriptions of early rising and vigorous exercise wouldn't do, Ross continued. "We had a rather merry Xmas & New Year, and I tried to dance my complaint 'down the wind'. But . . . I rather made things worse."

On June 27, 1844 Ross died a particularly excruciating death. Roderick Finlayson, the young man who served as Ross' second-in-command at Fort Victoria, was with him during his last hours. Of all the medicines Finlayson managed to force through Ross' tightly clenched jaws, only a mixture of brandy and water remained on his stomach.

"He departed this life," Finlayson wrote, "after a severe illness of five days, during which he was in a state of extreme torture, arising from a constipation of the bowels, accompanied by cold sweats, and violent spasms."[8] (*site 32*)

After Ross' death, Roderick Finlayson assumed command and, even though by then the fort may well have been all but complete, Finlayson must have found his new responsibilities onerous. He was just twenty-six and had been with the company only a few years. And while none doubted the sterling quality of his character, he was "never accounted a man of outstanding brilliancy."[9]

Soon after taking Ross' place, Finlayson found himself dealing with a serious confrontation with the otherwise friendly Songhees. In March of 1843, Douglas had informed the Songhees of his intention of building at Camosack. This news, Douglas reported, had "appeared to please them very much."[10]

"They immediately offered their services in procuring pickets for the establishment, an offer which I gladly accepted, and promised to pay them a Blanket for every forty pickets of 22 feet by 36 inches which they bring."

Having supplied the Company with the pickets which would form the palisade designed to keep them out of the fort, the Songhees had moved from their village at Cadboro Bay and settled agreeably beside the gully near the fort.

Other than "shewing their dexterity at light fingered work," the Songhees had caused no serious trouble until, in 1844, Finlayson discovered that they had killed some of the Company's oxen which had been allowed to roam freely outside the fort. Finlayson called the chief to the fort and demanded payment."[11]

"He went away in a rage," Finlayson noted, "and the next move I found on their part was a shower of bullets fired at the fort, with a great noise and demonstration on the part of the crowd assembled threatening death and devastation to all whites."

Ordering the bastion manned, Finlayson directed the fort's nine-pounder at the chief's lodge. One carefully aimed blast and the lodge exploded, filling the air with flying splinters.

Unhurt but recognizing an object lesson when he saw one, the chief approached the fort and after brief negotiations, during which Finlayson promised to level the entire village unless the oxen were paid for, agreed to the Company's terms.

Having settled this matter to his satisfaction, Finlayson was prepared for a second confrontation which occurred a short time later. A fire had broken out near the Songhees village and had threatened to spread through the woods to the fort. The Company men managed to put out the fire but only, Finlayson said, with "some difficulty." To avoid a second occurrence Finlayson ordered the Songhees to remove their village to the other side of the harbour. The Indians objected, pointing out with undeniable logic that the land was theirs and they could live where they liked. Finlayson won them over by agreeing to assign the Company's men to help dismantle their lodges and ferry them across the harbour.

RODERICK FINLAYSON. *Finlayson assumed command of Fort Victoria after Charles Ross' death. In 1878 he was elected Mayor of Victoria and by 1891 was one of the largest property owners in the city.*

9

Finlayson continued Ross' efforts to meet the Company-set goal for self-sufficiency. The fort had been supplied with food for its first year but after that it was expected to see to its own needs. Two dairies were established, each with seventy half-wild cows sent from the Company fort at Nisqually (near Tacoma). By 1847 almost three hundred acres were under cultivation — at the fort farm which covered much of the present business district and at Beckley Farm in today's James Bay residential district. Wheat, peas and potatoes were produced in such abundance that the Company was able to begin exporting vegetables to the Russian fur-traders at Sitka on the Alaskan coast.

SOUTH-WEST BASTION. *The nine-pounder housed in the fort's south-west bastion claimed only one victim. Charles Fish died after his arm was blown off when the cannon was fired to celebrate the arrival of the immigrant ship* Tory *in 1851.*

In 1846 the Oregon Boundary Treaty fixed the 49th parallel as the boundary between American and British possessions in the west. Now that it was in American territory, plans were prepared to abandon Fort Vancouver. Fort Victoria, which would now become Company headquarters, was enlarged. In 1849 James Douglas was transferred from the Columbia to become Chief Factor and trader-in-charge of the establishment.

3.
"a life of soul-improving simplicity"

Once in residence in the Chief Factor's house, Douglas set high standards of social behaviour for the officers of the fort. The military-like organization of the HBC clearly separated the officers who were chiefly Scots, from the enlisted men, the 'labouring class' of French Canadians and half-breeds, and the Kanakas who had been recruited at the Company's post in the Hawaiian Islands. Only officers were invited to join Douglas for supper — an all-male affair with Amelia and her daughters flitting in from the kitchen to serve the men who sat around a table spread with white linen and set with silver and sparkling crystal.

In the interests of avoiding undue levity, Douglas came prepared with conversational topics of suitable seriousness, gleaned from months-old copies of English newspapers. The Chief Factor met any attempt to venture into the frivolous with a stern stare. And it was with some relief when, supper over, the officers escaped to their own quarters, the Bachelors' Hall, to enjoy a pipe, to savour more than a few post-prandial brandies and to unwittingly provide entertainment for the children of the fort's school who were lodged in the room above.

Peering down from the vantage point provided by a loose and easily moved floor board, the students viewed "the mild orgies of the bachelors; oysters, sherry, port and brandy in abundance."[12]

The school, operated by the Company for the children of the officers posted at Fort Victoria and on the mainland, was run by the Reverend Robert John Staines. Twenty-seven years old and a graduate of Cambridge, Staines was teaching in France when he learned that the Company was attempting to recruit a schoolmaster for Fort Victoria. On discovering that the schoolmaster was expected to double as the fort's chaplain Staines rose to the occasion and allowed himself to be "prevailed upon" to take holy orders.

When Staines and his wife Emma arrived at the fort on March 17, 1849, they were appalled by the conditions they found. Roderick Finlayson was forced to lay planks in advance of Mrs. Staines' progress so that she could keep her skirts out of the mud as she made her way from the ship to the fort.

"They looked around wonderingly at the bare walls of the buildings and expressed deep surprise," Finlayson remembered.

Under the supervision of Staines and his wife, the children who boarded at the school lived a life of soul-improving simplicity quite devoid of unchristian comforts.

Their dormitory in the attic of the Bachelors' Hall was heated only by the air that circulated from the rooms below. In winter it often became so cold that water froze in the pitchers and the students went to bed unwashed until the weather improved.

Their meals were certainly less appealing than those enjoyed by the officers. For breakfast they were served bread and treacle, and tea without milk.

FORT VICTORIA, *the Bachelors' Hall on the right and the Chief Factor's house on the left. The bell, hanging in the tall belfry near the center of the fort, was rung for rising and for meals, to mark the working hours and to announce Sunday services. Each peal of the bell was met by a chorus from the fort's dogs and an answering chorus from the dogs in the Songhees village across the harbour.*

A dinner of potatoes and meat or perhaps fish was following by an evening feast which repeated the breakfast menu. And if a child saved a crust to nibble on during the night he would find stiff competition from the rats that overran the dormitory.

Apples were strange fruit, available only when Amelia Douglas shared the supply she had ordered from Nisqually. Oranges and sugar cane were unexpected treats, occasionally delivered by ships' captains outbound from Hawaii.

When they were not enduring mind-numbing Sundays learning the Collects or school-days struggling with the declension of Latin verbs, the girls were taught to be English ladies by Emma Staines and the boys were allowed to amuse themselves. They hung aroung the blacksmith's shop where the smithy, a French Canadian known as Beauchamp, was famous for his "bloodcurdling bad language in French and English" which they found entered the memory much more readily than either the Collects or Latin. They endlessly discussed the rumour that a keg of rum was buried beneath the clump of oak trees near the south-west bastion. They played with marbles, hand-made of clay and fired by the blacksmith. They played rounders using a ball made out of hair and covered with deer hide and they whiled away happy hours "fighting Indian boys and worrying Indian dogs."

"A favourite amusement," one scholar recalled, "was catching dog fish and after fastening a billet of wood with about a foot of line to the tail, letting him go. It afforded us great joy to witness his futile attempts to escape."[13]

Some found Staines "a man full of frills" and most acknowledged that he was a lazy pedant. Douglas, who allowed that it might be possible to find a man *worse* qualified than Staines, saved his praise for Emma. "She is invaluable and receives less assistance than she ought from her husband, who is rather lazy at times."[14]

Emma Staines' mission in life was to civilize the traders' half-breed daughters placed in her care. She made sure they were neatly and correctly dressed. She saw that they carried themselves properly. She insisted that they pay attention to deportment. And, as the first white woman many of her pupils had encountered, she provided them with a glimpse of what the future might hold by scrupulously avoiding Amelia Douglas.

"She and Mrs. Staines did not chum at all," Amelia's son-in-law would recall years later, "there being too much uppishness about the latter, she being the great woman . . ."[15]

Douglas' admiration of Mrs. Staines may have demonstrated nothing more than an insensitivity to his wife's feelings. But it may be that he understood that decisions made a continent away threatened to disrupt the fort's society and that the girls might benefit from being prepared for the changes that would follow.

EMMA STAINES. *Emma left Fort Victoria in 1854 soon after her husband, the Reverend Robert Staines, died in a shipwreck. Carrying settlers' complaints to London, Staines had been trapped when his ship, overloaded with lumber, was caught in a storm off Cape Flattery. As the ship floundered broadside in the water Staines managed to cut his way through its side, but he died, clinging to the wreckage, a day or two before rescuers arrived.*

4.
"an officer and gentleman"

South of the 49th parallel there were vocal Americans whose continental ambitions had not been satisfied by the terms of the 1846 boundary treaty. They continued to insist that it was the "manifest destiny" of the United States to extend control of the continent to the Russian possessions at 54°40' North. While a great westward migration had resulted in rapid population growth in Washington and Oregon Territories, the British possessions north of the 49th remained an empty attic, populated only by indigenous peoples and a few dozen HBC employees.

Aware that American expansionists were being rallied by the call "Fifty-four forty or fight" and recognizing that it might prove impossible to exercise a paper claim to an empty land, the government in London developed a plan to encourage British emigration. In 1849 the Colony of Vancouver Island was formed and Fort Victoria, the only settlement on the island, became its capital.

Colonization schemes require some organizing body capable of parcelling out land and providing civic amenities, such as roads, bridges and schools. Being the only organization of any kind already in place, the HBC was charged with these responsibilities.

As manager of the Colony, the HBC was expected to encourage colonization. However the Company set conditions which tended to do the reverse. In Washington Territory land could be had simply by occupying it and filing a claim. But the Colony was to be financed by the monies realized from the sale of lands and furthermore, the Company feared that free land might lead to the establishment of hardscrabble farms whose proprietors lacked the capital to develop them into profitable enterprises. Therefore, to enrich colonial revenues and to promote the development of a local squirearchy — gentlemen farmers who would run large estates from substantial manor houses — the Company decreed that land would be sold only in one hundred acre parcels. Each acre would cost £1 and purchasers would be required to bring out from England one workman for every twenty acres they acquired. The Colony of Vancouver Island would, it was thought, attract only well-heeled, or at least financially solvent, colonists.

Captain Walter Colquhoun Grant, late of the Scots Greys and the first man who was not connected with the HBC to take up land on the Island, was flat broke when he reached Fort Victoria in August of 1849. After a bank failure had swept away his fortune, Grant, who admitted that his debts were "numerous" and his creditors "pressing", had been forced to sell his commission in the army.

"I think I shall have about £ 900 to begin my adventure with," Grant had cheerfully announced, confident that he would soon be able to make good on outstanding debts of some £ 4000 that he had left behind in England.[16]

His £ 900 spent long before he reached Fort Victoria, Grant's passage up the west coast was paid by the Company. It was an advance, rather than a loan, Grant insisted. The Company had contracted him to act as Colonial Surveyor and Grant suggested that the Company simply deduct from his annual salary of £100 whatever they spent on his behalf.

Grant had brought with him what he considered necessities of life for a gentleman farmer — cricket sets, a fancy carriage harness, a personal library and two small cannons of polished brass with which to ornament his estate. The Company was forced to provide him with incidentals — the food which would keep Grant and his workmen alive during their first winter and the oxen, cattle and horses which would stock his farm.

Grant, one HBC man grumbled, exhibited a "flightiness" that approached "near lunacy."[17]

But flightiness alone did not account for Grant's failure to become a successful farmer. Soon after he arrived he made the daunting discovery that the HBC had reserved for its own use some twenty to thirty square miles of the best agricultural land closest to the fort and Grant was forced to choose his acres at Sooke, twenty miles distant from protection and provisions.

By September of 1849 Grant and his men were working determinedly to get a roof over their heads before winter. Grant's little cabin of squared logs, approached by a grandly curving carriage drive and defended by his little brass cannons, was christened 'Mullachard' after his ancestral home in Scotland.

"The house was a shanty," one visitor recalled.[18]

'MULLACHARD'. *Captain Grant's Sooke farmhouse was stuffed with books, sporting rifles and expensive furniture. Expecting to live the life of a gentleman, Grant had arrived from England with all manner of useless items, including the set of cricket bats and wickets which he generously, but perhaps rather forlornly, presented to the boys at the fort's school.*

The Company, desperate for the accurate surveys needed before land sales could proceed, nagged at Grant to get to work. It came as something of a surprise to the Captain, whose only experience with surveying was a nodding acquaintance he had made with the subject at the Royal Military College at Sandhurst, to discover that he was expected to accomplish the surveying himself, rather than leading a party of experienced men. Often required to hack his way through thick bush to clear a line of sight, Grant compounded his problems by lacking a sense of direction. On one occasion after he had set out from 'Mullachard' for Fort Victoria, Grant lost his way and was found five days later in very bad shape having been without food and water since his departure.[19]

After completing only a few surveys, notable for their lack of accuracy, Grant resigned his position as Colonial Surveyor in March of 1850. He had fired half of his workmen for misconduct and the remainder were threatening to desert to the goldfields of California. All of his attention, Grant insisted was required on his own estate.

"I have been living a totally solitary existence," Grant informed a relative in Scotland. "I soon got tired of my own society & except when a stray ship came along the coast, never saw a creature save my own men and a few rascally Indians."[20]

To relieve his loneliness, Grant trudged the twenty-five miles to the fort where, personable and amusing, he was a welcome addition to the festivities in the Bachelors' Hall. An excellent swordsman, Grant, when in his cups, could easily be prevailed upon to demonstrate his skill. But he found no volunteers when after snuffing a candle with one sweep of his sword and then splitting it down the middle with another, he announced that he could remove the buttons from a wearer's coat with equal steadiness.

On one riotous occasion, Grant announced that the Queen was leaving Buckingham Palace for Windsor Castle and that the Company officers were to serve as her calvary-escort. "Down everybody went," a reveller reported.[21] With Grant in the lead, they hopped about the Hall kangaroo fashion until, disturbed from sleep in her dormitory overhead, a schoolgirl doused their good humour with a carefully aimed pitcherful of water.

Despite such pleasant diversions, Grant found himself weary of his existence and contemplating suicide by the autumn of 1850. A pioneer in discovering a satisfactory antidote to winter depression, Grant hopped aboard a ship bound for the HBC trading post in Hawaii where he spent two months warming himself in the sun and, according to local tradition, collecting the broom seeds which he planted on his return, introducing the yellow-flowered shrub that has now spread throughout the lower Island.

"I returned from the Islands with fresh vigour," Grant reported. But soon the apparent hopelessness of his situation closed in on him. He rented out his farm, signing over all the proceeds to the Hudson's Bay Company to defray his debts which now amounted to over £ 400 and in the summer of 1851 quit the Colony to try his luck in Oregon.

Two years later a former acquaintance found him working as a longshoreman on the San Francisco docks. Struggling to keep body and soul together, talking rather wildly about going to Mexico "to try what can be done there," Grant was hoping to put together enough money to pay his passage to Vancouver Island so that he could sell his farm to finance further adventures.

"After all the experience he has had, he is yet so d_____ extravagant that I will probably have to pay his passage," his friend predicted.[22] A month later, in September of 1853, Grant reappeared in the Colony, arranged for the sale of his property and departed before the year was out.

Grant returned to England and rejoined his old regiment. He fought in the Crimea and at the time of the Mutiny was sent to India where he died of dysentery on August 27, 1861 at the age of thirty-nine.

"A splendid fellow and every inch an officer and gentleman," Grant was fondly remembered on Vancouver Island. Gregarious and possessing an irresistible charm, he left behind many bad debts but no bad feelings. He possessed, one creditor sighed, "a peculiar talent for getting into the pockets of his friends."[23]

5.
"a great smoker"

In drafting the royal charter of 1849, which created the Colony of Vancouver Island, the Colonial Office had reserved to the Crown the right to appoint the colonial governor. Given the power to raise and command a militia, the governor was also empowered to appoint a seven-member council and to arrange for the election of a general assembly. With the advice and consent of these two bodies, the governor was to enact all laws and ordinances required for the "Peace, Order and good Government" of the colony.[24]

The first governor arrived at Fort Victoria on March 9, 1850. A graduate of both Oxford and Cambridge, Richard Blanshard was an ambitious young barrister who hoped that his performance as Governor of Vancouver Island would lead to more prestigious appointments. But he was deeply disappointed by the conditions he discovered in the colony and must soon have come to suspect that his tenure on the Island might mark the end, rather than the beginning, of a successful vice-regal career.

He was "rather startled by the wild aspect of the country," Douglas observed.[25] A reaction that may have been compounded by the fact that a foot of snow lay on the ground when Blanshard stepped ashore to read the proclamation announcing his appointment to a discouragingly small assembly of naval officers and HBC employees.

Although his arrival had been expected, his residence had not been completed. Forced to spend the first month of his governorship living aboard the Royal Navy ship *Driver* and later given a room in the fort, Blanshard noted impatiently that the construction of his house ranked low on Douglas' list of priorities.

Work on British Columbia's first Government House had begun in

17

February, 1850, a month before Blanshard arrived. But Douglas often diverted the builders to projects he considered more important.

"I find that three of the Kanakas and one of the workmen have been withdrawn from my cottage, leaving one solitary man to carry on work that has already been loitered over for more than five months," Blanshard informed Douglas in August.[26] Another month passed before Douglas was able to report that the house was "nearly finished".

Built on a site a few hundred feet north of the fort, the governor's premises consisted of one building of eight hundred square feet with an attached kitchen and a smaller house for his servants. (*site 22*)

Douglas felt that the governor's house had "a neat appearance" and was "the best finished building" in the Colony. An assessment with which Blanshard apparently did not agree for he spent $700, almost half the amount the house had cost, improving it.[27]

RICHARD BLANSHARD. *The first Governor of Vancouver Island, Richard Blanshard wrote to London requesting a recall within months of arriving at Fort Victoria.*

"A great smoker" and "a great sportsman", Blanshard had impressed the HBC men with his quiet gentlemanly manner and his lack of hauteur and pomposity. But, however appealing Blanshard's personal attributes might be, the Company men felt that they owed their loyalty to Chief Factor Douglas rather than the newly arrived governor.

Blanshard found himself in the invidious position of governing a colony which could boast of only one bona-fide colonist and which had produced no revenues to support a colonial governor. He had been led to understand that, rather than receiving a salary, he would be given a one thousand acre estate. Upon arriving on Vancouver Island, he learned that not only were there no available farm labourers to work his lands but also the estate went with the office and any revenues it might produce were his only so long as his term as governor lasted. On November 18, 1850 Blanshard wrote to the Colonial Office, resigning as governor and citing his dwindling purse and his poor health as the reasons for requesting a recall.

Suffering agonies from tic douloureux and plagued by recurring bouts of malaria, Blanshard was forced to wait ten months before the despatch relieving him of his duties arrived from London. He spent much of the time lying in his bed nursing his complaints with morphine and writing despatches critical of the HBC's colonization policies.

Land prices were too high, Blanshard claimed. One or two Company servants had purchased small plots near the fort, but others who might have been willing to settle were deterred by the price. The thousands of acres the Company had reserved for its own use discouraged settlement as few would choose to live so far from the fort. And furthermore, Blanshard stated, no townsite had been mentioned, let alone selected. The policies pursued by the HBC tended to "exclude free Settlers, and reserve the Island either as an enlarged Post of their own, or a desert," he concluded.[28]

The governor was not alone in blaming the HBC for the colony's slow development. But even if settlers had flooded in, it seems unlikely that southern Vancouver Island would have become the site of a prosperous agriculturally based colony, for even the Company's own farms, which suffered from few of the disadvantages cited by Blanshard, cannot be seen as having been successful.

6.
"such a state of inconvenience"

Beckley Farm in James Bay and later Uplands Farm in north Oak Bay together with the Company's two dairies had been established by the HBC simply to sustain the fort. But after 1849, when the Company was charged with promoting colonization, a new farm policy was called for — one that encouraged immigration and viewed farms as profitable enterprises.

A joint stock company, the Puget Sound Agricultural Company, was formed in London. The PSAC, whose shareholders were almost exclusively HBC officers, would abide by the colonial land polices set by the Company, thus proving them to be workable, and would attempt to replicate on Vancouver Island institutions which had proved successful in Britain.

PSAC farms would be managed by a bailiff who would assume the role of a country squire. The bailiffs, drawn from the gentleman-farmer class, would receive a small salary and a share of the profits earned by their farms. Labourers, indentured servants who signed a five-year contract to work the farms would, when their contracts expired, be granted twenty-acre holdings and would become, it was hoped, a class of stalwart yeomanry.

Four farms, Viewfield, Constance Cove, Colwood and Craigflower, were established within the Fur Trade Reserve. They were all large farms, from six hundred to one thousand acres, and every effort was made to ensure their success, but none of them existed, at least as they had been planned, ten years after they had first been formed.

Viewfield, established in 1850, was the first to begin operations and the only PSAC farm to be managed by a former HBC officer rather than a bailiff

19

recruited in England or Scotland. Donald Macauley, a "long and spare" Highlander, operated Viewfield principally as a sheep station.

In 1851 Captain Edward Edwards Langford arrived to assume management of Colwood Farm. Captain Langford had sold his commission in the army some years earlier and had taken up farming in the south of England. When he found himself somewhat impoverished after a will from which he had expected to benefit was discovered to have been unsigned, he decided to sign on with the PSAC to try his luck in a new colony.

COLWOOD FARM. *Managed by bailiff Captain Edward Langford and built in 1851 on land now occupied by the Royal Colwood Golf Club, Colwood became the scene of many happy evenings, made merry by Langford's lavish hospitality, by his possession of the only piano in the Colony and by the presence of his five daughters.*

In 1853 the last bailiffs arrived. Thomas Skinner, who was to manage Constance Cove Farm, was a native of Essex. As a young man he had sailed to Calcutta and Rangoon in the employ of the East India Company. Married and with a young family, Skinner was prepared to settle down and the contract offered by the PSAC allowed him to combine responsibility with a certain amount of adventure.

Kenneth McKenzie was a Scot and the most experienced farmer of the four bailiffs. Appointed the general overseer of all PSAC farms, McKenzie was also given responsibility for Craigflower. (*site 58*) The largest of the four farms, Craigflower had been assigned a key role by the PSAC. Not only would the farm become self-sufficient, manufacturing its own bricks and producing lumber, but it would also provide other farms with those commodities.

Langford, Skinner and McKenzie would all later claim that the Company had misrepresented the conditions they would find on their arrival. James

Douglas, who had spent his adult life in the wilderness and whose standards of comfort were rather different from those of the three bailiffs, was somewhat bemused by their complaints. But Charles Bayley, who had sailed to Victoria aboard the *Tory* arriving with the Langfords in 1851, agreed with the bailiffs.

Bayley's father had been contracted to manage Uplands Farm for the HBC. When they arrived at the farm they were shown two unfinished log cabins which the HBC had prepared to accommodate the Bayleys and the seventeen men in their employ.

"Window glass unknown, some used oiled paper instead. Furniture none, round logs for seats, bunks for bedsteads, deer, bear and sheep skins for carpet, bugs innumerable, fleas without limit," Bayley grumbled. "Four miles from the fort and our only protection shotguns and dogs."[29]

Captain Langford, who had been accompanied by his family, refused to inhabit the two small cabins provided for him at Colwood. Instead he insisted on living near the fort until an acceptable home was built for him. He was directed to a small, one-roomed log hut which stood just outside the fort gates and into this he crowded his five daughters and very pregnant wife.

Richard Blanshard was still biding his time waiting for his official release when the Langfords arrived in 1851. Declaring himself to be "extremely sorry to see an English lady reduced to such a state of inconvenience," he offered them rooms in his own house until after Flora Langford delivered her baby.

When Skinner, his wife and five small children arrived in 1853, they were directed to a loft above one of the fort's buildings. Douglas, who had considered similar accommodations quite adequate for schoolchildren, must have thought Skinner overly fastidious when he rejected the attic room, but deciding to humour him, he allowed him to use a cabin which had housed some of the Company's Hawaiian servants along Kanaka road (Humboldt Street). A month after their arrival, Skinner's wife gave birth, shielded by a blanket which had been strung across a rope to divide the single room in two.

Kenneth McKenzie, appalled by the housing offered to him and his family, threatened to reboard the ship that had carried him from England and sail for home, preferring an additional six months aboard ship to the squalor of Fort Victoria. He was persuaded to stay only after Douglas had horses saddled and took him to see the site of his farm. Won over by the beauty of the Gorge and Portage Inlet, McKenzie decided to stay.

With the McKenzies and the Skinners had come seventy-three labourers and tradesmen, most of them recruited in Scotland, and some of them accompanied by their wives. A few independent settlers had ventured to the Island but, because the Company had not loosened its grip on the Fur Trade Reserve, they, like Captain Grant, had been forced to settle at Metchosin or Sooke.

Although immigration had been slow, the HBC had gradually sold a few small plots near the fort and a little village had begun to develop. In 1852 the townsite of Victoria was laid out in streets and by 1854, seventy-nine houses had been built close to the fort and the population of the town, including the officers and men of the fort, had reached 232.[30]

Outside the town's boundaries to the north and east were cultivated fields divided by only a few roads or trails. One led over a bridge to the Songhees village and on to Macauley's farm and from there to Craigflower and Colwood. Another led away from the eastern gate of the fort, towards John Tod's property at the Willows and the HBC's Uplands Farm at the northern end of Oak Bay. A pathway wound around James Bay, crossed a plank which had been thrown across the little brook at the head of the bay, and then meandered along the southern shore through groves of arbutus, maple and oak, past clumps of mock orange and red-flowering currant and on to Laurel Point where the ground was carpeted with white lilies and other wild flowers.

James Douglas, having decided to make Victoria his permanent home, had built his house on James Bay's southern shore in 1851. (*site 2*) Considered "a very grand affair and the most up-to-date . . . in the Colony," Douglas' home was two stories high with deep, sheltered verandahs and a roof line broken by several dormers. Rather than the simple planking which covered the inner walls of other buildings, the walls of Douglas' house were plastered, the lime for the plaster made from clam shells collected by the Songhees.[31]

JAMES DOUGLAS HOUSE. *Built in 1851 on the shores of James Bay, Douglas' residence survived until 1906 when its contents were sold at auction and the house was demolished.*

On December 27, 1852 Dr. John Sebastian Helmcken, a twenty-seven year old London-trained physician who had joined the HBC in 1849 and arrived at Fort Victoria the following year, married Douglas' seventeen year old daughter Cecilia.

On the day of their wedding two feet of snow lay on the ground and Cecilia who had been expecting the arrival of a two wheeled cart, "the only thing approaching to a carriage" in the colony, was collected instead by a makeshift sleigh, a wooden packing crate fastened atop willow runners. With a tinkle of sleigh bells it set off across the snow, around the head of James Bay carrying Cecilia to the Bachelors' Hall and her waiting bridegroom. After the

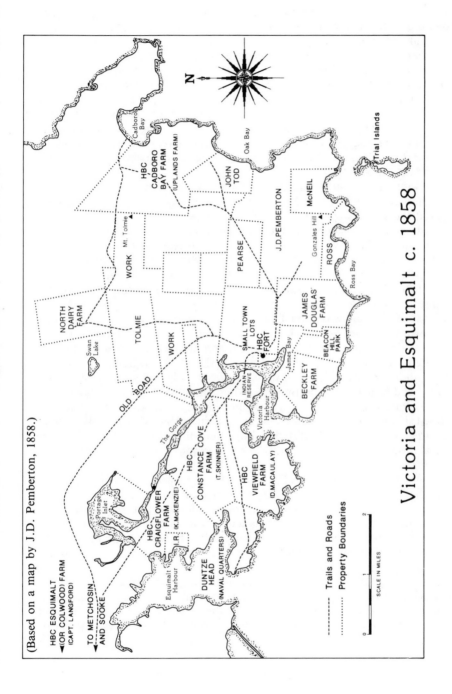

(Based on a map by J.D. Pemberton, 1858.)

Victoria and Esquimalt c. 1858

Trails and Roads
Property Boundaries

SCALE IN MILES

23

wedding, the guns in the bastions roared, the fort's bell clanged, the dogs howled and all the men fired muskets in celebration. With grog served out all around, the day became one of "feasting, revelling and jollity."[32]

Perhaps reluctant to part with Cecilia and wanting Helmcken close by to protect his family during his absences, Douglas gave the couple an acre of land adjacent to his own house. (*site 3*) The Helmcken's house was thirty by thirty-five feet, built by French Canadians out of logs that had been squared in the forest where they were felled, brought to the beach in front of the house by water and hauled to the site by oxen. The roof was shingled with split cedar shakes, provided by the Songhees in return for HBC blankets and the floor planked with rough, uneven boards, almost a foot wide, cut by Kanakas in a saw-pit.[33]

By 1854, the only settlement in the James Bay area, other than the Douglas and Helmcken houses, was Beckley Farm where the four young men who worked the 120 cleared acres lived in two small farmhouses. To the east, through tangles of blackberry and wild rose and past Beacon Hill and Clover Point where wild clover a foot high waved and rippled with the on-shore breezes, was the Ross' hundred- acre farm, where Isabella, the widow of Charles Ross, struggled to support her children. Along the northern boundary of Ross' farm was Gonzalo, the two hundred acre holding which would form the nucleus of Joseph Despard Pemberton's Gonzales estate. North and east of Gonzalo was John Tod's four hundred acre farm (*site 61*) which ran down to the beach at Oak Bay and shared its northern boundary with the HBC's Uplands Farm which sprawled over eleven hundred acres and was operated principally as a sheep station. To the west of Uplands Farm were four hundred acres which Dr. William Fraser Tolmie had decided to buy in 1852 and which would become his retirement home a few years later. Between Tolmie's land and the waters of the Gorge, John Work and his family farmed six hundred acres. Like Tod and Tolmie, Work was an HBC officer and all three had been permitted to buy land within the Fur Trade Reserve and without importing the farm workers required by truly independent settlers.

A census compiled by James Douglas in 1854 revealed that the total population of all these farms amounted to no more than seventy men, women and children. The PSAC farms were home to an additional 154 individuals, over sixty of whom were children under fifteen. The independent settlers in Sooke and Metchosin numbered only seventeen adults: the Muirs, who had bought Grant's acres in Sooke, and in Metchosin, the middle-aged Blinkhorns and their niece, Martha Cheney.

The entire adult population of the town of Victoria and its outlying farms was just over three hundred. But even in so small a community, class divisions had begun to appear. The arrival of the McKenzies, the Skinners, and particularly the Langfords began to change the simple fur trade society of the colony.

7.

"if they would only learn to wear a crinoline properly"

A division of classes had, of course, existed when the only people on the Island were HBC men and their wives. Company officers, most of whom were Scots and many of whom were well-educated, formed the upper class. The lower orders were the French Canadians, half-breeds and Kanakas — the axemen, blacksmiths and manual workers who made up the Company's labouring class.

Men like John Work and John Tod, as retired HBC officers, understood this social arrangement and fitted into it very well. But people who had come to the colony direct from Britain viewed the traders and their half-breed wives as something lower than society's upper crust. Even James Douglas, who had been appointed Governor after Blanshard's departure, did not escape the scorn of some of the newcomers.

Annie Deans, semi-literate and the wife of an indentured servant at Craigflower, clearly thought herself superior to the Governor.

"The Governor of Vancouver Island has been in the Company out here ever since he was a Boy about 15 year and now is a Man upwards of 60 now — so you may say he has been all his life among North American indians and has got one of them for a wife so how can it be expected that he can know anything at all about Governing one of England's last Colony's in North America," Annie wrote to her family in Scotland.[34]

And Douglas, as well as occupying a position of power, had been married to Amelia for many years, unlike Work and Tod whose casual 'country' arrangements with their spouses had only been recently formalized.

An Irishman, John Work was born in 1792 and had spent his entire adult life working for the HBC. In 1852 soon after he retired from the Company, he purchased the seven hundred acres that made up Hillside Farm and devoted himself to raising pumpkins that weighed over one hundred pounds and all manner of equally impressive fruits and vegetables.

In 1826, Work had 'married' Josette Legace, the daughter of a French Canadian voyageur and a Spokane Indian woman. Wherever he went he took Josette with him and fifteen years after their union he continued to regard her with fondness.

"The little wife and I get on very well," he wrote in 1841. "She is to me an affectionate partner simple and uninstructed as she is and takes good care of my children & myself."[35]

Taking care of the children was no small task, for by 1841 Josette had already given birth to eight of the eleven children she would bear during their years together. When the Works settled at Hillside, five of their daughters were in their teens. John's "kindly disposition", Josette's French sparkle, and a houseful of young women combined to make Hillside Farm something of a social centre.

Charles Wilson, a young lieutenant in the party of Royal Engineers who had been sent to survey the boundary line between American and British possessions, visited the Works often during the time he was encamped at Esquimalt.

HILLSIDE FARM. *John Work's Hillside farmhouse was located within the area now bounded by Quadra, Cook, Hillside and Bay Streets.*

"The Works are about the kindest people I ever came across," he wrote in his journal. " 'My western home' I call it."[36]

To get to the Works, Wilson had to ride six miles there and six miles back, often through mud up to his horse's girth. But the trip was worth it. Dropping in at Hillside one New Years Day, Wilson received typical Work hospitality.

"There were about 30 at dinner," he wrote, "nearly all of the family & a regular good old English one it was, such a display of fish, flesh, fowl and pastry as is seldom seen. We danced until 12 & then all hands sat down to a sumptuous supper & then set to work dancing again until a very late hour."

Wilson found much to admire at the Works, but he particularly noted the girls' equestrian skill.

"The young ladies are first rate horse women & sit with an ease & gracefulness (very seldom seen at home) even when at a full gallop."

But he was aware that not all Englishmen in the colony felt the same way he did.

"Many English people, most of a rather questionable standing at home, have come out here & pretend to look down upon the old settlers," he wrote. But even Wilson, while pledging his loyalty to his friends, had to admit that the Works would not have been his friends had they met in England. Despite himself, he could not help making comparisons.

"The ladies here are nicely dressed . . . though they would look much better if they would only learn to wear a crinoline properly. It is most lamentable to see the objects they make of themselves, some of the hoops being quite oval, whilst others had only one hoop rather high up, the remainder of the dress hanging down perpendicularly."

When he decided to settle in the colony, John Work realized that his children would have to cope with a society very different from the one he and Josette had enjoyed and when his two oldest daughters announced that they planned to marry, Work decided to legitimize them. After living as man and wife for almost twenty-five years, he and Josette were married before the Reverend Staines on November 6, 1849, just five weeks before their daughter Sarah married Roderick Finlayson and three months before Jane married Dr. Tolmie.

John Tod also found it desirable to enter belatedly into wedlock made holy by a minister's presence. Born in Scotland in 1794, Tod was, with the exception of John Work, the oldest man in the colony but the last of his four wives was providing him with one of the youngest families.

JOHN TOD. An "antiquarian pensioner", John Tod was the first person to choose Victoria as a retirement home. His farmhouse, completed in 1851 and the oldest residence in western Canada is alleged to be haunted.

Tod's first liason had been with Catherine Birstone, an Indian girl he had met when he was stationed near Lake Winnipeg. Five years after Catherine gave birth to his son James in 1818, Tod was transferred to New Caledonia. He left Catherine and James behind and while he remained distantly concerned about James, he wasted no time fretting about Catherine's well-being.

"I wish to God I had him with me, tho not his mother," he confided to a friend.[37]

By 1826, the same year he learned that Catherine had come under the protection of another trader, Tod found himself a second companion who enlivened his evenings by singing accompaniment when he played his flute and by providing him with at least one child. Like her predecessor she was left behind in 1834 when Tod was granted leave to return to Scotland for a visit.

On the voyage to England, he met Eliza Waugh, a Welshwoman in her mid-twenties who was returning home after spending five years working at the Red River settlement for a clergyman and his wife. Tod and Eliza were

27

married in London and she returned with him to a lonely fur-trade post where, on December 3, 1835 their daughter Emmeline Jane was born.

Eliza's mind seems to have been rather delicately balanced and Tod's fellow traders had wondered at his marrying a "half Cracked Brainid Chamber Maid".[38] Childbirth combined with months in a dreary wilderness, tipped the scales and by the summer of 1837 Tod was forced to admit that he had a madwoman on his hands. Given special leave by the Company, Tod took Eliza home to Wales where he deposited her with her mother. Diagnosed as "a confirmed lunatic," Eliza was placed in an asylum where she remained until she died in 1857.[39]

In 1843 or 1844 when he was stationed near Kamloops, Tod took his fourth and last wife. Sophia Lolo was an Indian girl, born in the North West. In her late teens when she first took up with Tod, she was at least thirty years his junior.

SOPHIA TOD. *The last of John Tod's four wives, Sophia Lolo.*

Like John Work, Tod had decided to settle near Victoria when he retired from the Company's service in 1850. (*site 61*) But unlike Work who took to farming with energetic enthusiasm, Tod seemed content to squat on his acres without improving them.

"The poor old gentleman is not very enterprising," Douglas noted.[40]

Tod was, it seems, conserving his energies for other activities. During their years at Oak Bay, Sophia increased the total of Tod's offspring to nine by giving birth to five children.

When his legal wife, Eliza, died in 1857, Tod was free to marry but he postponed his nuptials until 1863, a few months before his daughter Mary married John Bowker.

More than a desire to legitimize his daughter had prompted Tod's trip to the altar. In 1863 Tod's first companion turned up in Victoria. Catherine had come to the colony not to exercise a prior claim to Tod but to be close to their son James, who had married Flora, the daughter of Donald Macauley, bailiff of Viewfield Farm, and who had settled on a small holding near Mount

Douglas. Supporting herself by attending confinements and by dispensing folk medicines, Catherine was, nonetheless, making things rather awkward for her former cohabitant by calling herself 'Mrs. Tod' and by being addressed as such by all who knew her. By marrying Sophia, Tod removed from his daughter the taint of illegitimacy and also established the identity of the real Mrs. Tod.

When Langford departed Vancouver Island in 1861, he would be credited, or blamed, with having "done much to soften the rude features of pioneer life" and "to give the tone of modern English society to the colony."[41] Once his farmhouse was completed, Captain Langford had begun to behave in a manner he thought appropriate to a country gentleman. He took very seriously his responsibilities as host and entertained with a generosity that the Company, which was covering his living expenses until his farm began to produce, found lavish if not profligate. Company officers down whose throats disappeared a goodly share of the 237 pounds of tea and 70 gallons of brandy, whisky and wine consumed by the Langfords in 1853, admitted to feeling guilty when accepting his hospitality but struggled to enjoy themselves nonetheless.

CAPTAIN EDWARD E. LANGFORD. *When Langford returned to England in 1861, he was credited with having introduced the tone of modern English society to the Colony — a feat he accomplished by over-extending his credit with the HBC, in some years spending more than eight times his annual salary.*

Even more magnetic than his open-handed hospitality were Langford's wife Flora and their five teenaged daughters. Flora Langford had brought with her the first piano to appear in the colony and a piano combined with the most marriageable English girls to be found within a thousand miles were reason enough for lonely young men to beat a path to their door.

Many of those young men were officers in Her Majesty's Navy for soon after the Langford's arrival a distant war would suggest to the Admiralty that the harbour at Esquimalt might have a strategic importance and the officers and men of the Royal Navy would come to have an increasing importance to Victoria's economic and social life.

29

8.
"riff-raff excluded"

A British naval presence had existed in the Pacific since 1837. In that year a naval base had been established in Valparaiso, Chile, to protect trade routes to the Hawaiian Islands and Australia. Ships of the Royal Navy had begun calling at Fort Victoria soon after its construction in 1843 and while some officers complained that the Company charged unpatriotically high prices for the supplies they purchased, others recognized that the harbour at Esquimalt was excellent and that British possessions in the North Pacific could be better protected from American aggression by a naval base at Esquimalt than by a fleet stationed at faraway Valparaiso.

In 1854 Britain declared war on Russia and while most military attention was directed to the Black Sea and the Crimea, the Royal Navy's Pacific Fleet prepared to engage the enemy in the North Pacific by attacking the Russian fortifications at Petropavlosk on the Kamchatka Peninsula. On August 30, 1854 the attack was about to commence when the commander, Rear-Admiral David Price, his nerves giving way under the strain, committed suicide by shooting himself through the lungs. When the attack was finally launched five days later, the landing party, which included seven hundred marines and seamen, suffered heavy casualties — one-third of the men killed or wounded — and was easily repulsed by the Russian defenders.

On October 3, 1854 three ships involved in the Petropavlosk debacle entered the Esquimalt harbour. Tired and discouraged after the battle and the long voyage from the Kamchatka Peninsula and with their ships in need of repair, officers and men would have preferred to remain for a long recuperative stay. The harbour at Esquimalt was snug and safe. Wood and water were available on its shores and from Colwood and Craigflower farms, provisions could be obtained. But the ships carried eighty seamen wounded in the battle and few medical supplies and no hospital facilities were to be found in the colony. Reluctantly the small fleet sailed on October 16 for San Francisco.

On February 14, 1855 Sir Henry Bruce, Price's successor, wrote to Douglas warning him to be prepared for a visit by three or four ships in July. They would require, Bruce wrote, a good supply of coal and a full supply of fresh meat and vegetables, and, because they intended to launch a second attack on Petropavlosk, a building that could serve as a temporary hospital should be prepared.[42]

On May 8, Douglas responded, promising that the coal would be on hand, that two thousand sheep had been ordered from Nisqually and that he had urged the colony's residents to "use every exertion in raising vegetables." And, Douglas continued he would "take immediate steps for the erection of decent and comfortable buildings to serve as a naval hospital."[43]

Douglas had been anxious to accommodate the navy on two counts. As a trader he was aware that the navy had the potential to become a good and reliable consumer of the colony's products. And as governor he recognized that without the protection of Her Majesty's ships, Vancouver Island would remain vulnerable to future attack from both the Russians and the Americans. The more the navy came to rely on Esquimalt the better.

On a seven acre parcel of land on Duntze Head at the entrance to Esquimalt harbour — a site later described as "most unsuitable" and calculated to "encourage and invite" a shelling — Douglas ordered the construction of three hospital buildings. Rather than the temporary or makeshift structures suggested by the navy, the "Crimea huts" as they came to be known, were substantial buildings costing £ 932 and including kitchens, an operating room and surgeon's quarters.

CRIMEA HUTS. *The first buildings erected at the Esquimalt Naval Station.*

The navy's raid on Petropavlosk proved anti-climactic for the attackers found the stronghold deserted by the Russians and rather than accommodating dozens of wounded, the Crimea huts were used for the hospitalization of only one seaman who was suffering, not from wounds, but from scurvy. However, the importance of Esquimalt had been recognized and as more and more ships of the Pacific fleet began calling at the harbour and the colonists did all they could to welcome the sailors, the Admiralty was gradually convinced to abandon Valparaiso as its Pacific headquarters in favour of Esquimalt. In 1865 what had become a reality in practice was officially sanctioned when an Order-in-Council passed in London created a Royal Navy Establishment at Esquimalt.

The effect of the navy's presence on the little settlement which was slowly growing on southern Vancouver Island was enormous. Not only did it provide a market for colonial goods, but it also had a marked impact on society. Over the years, as the make-up of the population shifted and changed with the floods and ripples of immigration, the navy and particularly its officers all but guaranteed that British values would predominate and that one's position in British 'society' would remain the yardstick of social success.

Young officers stationed at Esquimalt were pursued by Victoria girls who saw in them a chance to make a better marriage than they could have ever have hoped to make had their families remained in Britain. In England, women who worried about slipping past marriageable age and who had the good fortune to have a sister or other female relative married to an officer serving in India, often found familial affections so strong that they made the long voyage to the sub-continent for extended visits, visits which always seemed to coincide with the beginning of the Cold Weather Season and its four months of dances, balls, picnics and garden parties, attended by a wonderfully numerous array of marriage-minded young army officers quite desperate for the company of English ladies. Victoria girls found their naval counterparts — well-bred and often high-born young midshipmen, lieutenants and captains — delivered to their very doorsteps.

The arrival of a naval ship invariably occasioned a round of parties. During the second week of August, 1856 HMS *Monarch* and *Trincomalee* dropped anchor in Esquimalt harbour and the following month Governor Douglas hosted a ball at the fort with music provided by the ship's band of the *Monarch*. "A very pleasant party, kept up until 4 o'clock in the morning," Martha Cheney recorded in her diary.[45]

RIDING PARTY, CRAIGFLOWER. *Riding parties, like the one pictured here on the bridge below Craigflower farm, were popular forms of entertainment. Of all the PSAC farmhouses, Craigflower is the only one to have escaped demolition.*

But festivities did not end with the Governor's Ball. Riding parties collected at the Langfords, explored the countryside and paused to picnic or to call at farmhouses in Metchosin. Ships' officers, more than willing to return the hospitality they received, organized entertainments of their own. They gave dinner parties and dances aboard ship. They volunteered ships' bands to play at any celebratory occasion. They commandeered ships' boats to take Mrs. Langford and, perhaps more to the point, Mrs. Langford's daughters, for a tour of the harbour — an invitation the ladies accepted with pleasure although, since the most efficient method of travel from Esquimalt to the fort was by canoe, they already knew the harbour more intimately than they cared. But then few of those trips had ended with a picnic on Cole Island in the company of young men who were so eager to please.

Setting a pattern for the years to come, two of Langford's daughters married naval officers. Louisa Ellen, Langford's eldest daughter, was nineteen when her family settled at Colwood. A "first-class piano player," she married John Josling whom she had met when he was serving as a lieutenant aboard HMS *Thetis*. They had been married only six years when Josling, promoted to captain and serving on the China Station, was blown apart by a shell which struck the bridge of his ship during an attack on Kagosima, Japan on August 15, 1863.[46]

Emma, the third Langford daughter, married John Augustus Bull, master and senior surveyor on the HMS *Plumper*. The wedding took place on February 7, 1860 at Colwood, shortly before Bull left to spend the spring and summer surveying the coast. Soon after he returned to Esquimalt that fall, he accepted an invitation to dine at the naval hospital with the resident doctor. That night he became violently ill. He instantly vomited the dose of salts a desperate Emma administered to him and by the next morning he was in such pain that she sent for help. The doctor with whom he had spent the previous afternoon arrived to pronounce him dead. The local newspaper, aware that the sudden death of a naval man might be put down to intemperance, assure its readers that Bull was "noted for his correct and steady habits, and was much esteemed by his brother officers for his many virtues."

Not all unions of Victoria girls and naval officers ended so tragically. But few can be seen as having been entirely successful. A girlhood spent in Victoria did not guarantee an easy transition into English society and with family and friends far away women did not always find it easy to cope with often difficult and sometimes alcoholic officer-husbands. More successful were marriages between local girls and the HBC officers and colonial officials who made Victoria their home. Mary, Langford's second daughter, chose such a man and the years they spent together seem to have been happy and contented.

George Lewis was 23, the "not so agreeable" second mate of the *Tory*, the slow old-fashioned barque which had brought the Langfords to Fort Victoria in 1851. Seventeen year old Mary had attracted Lewis' attention on that voyage and after 1853 when he was appointed first officer of the HBC steamer *Otter* on the Company's coastal service, he had many opportunities to meet Mary at Colwood and at Martha Cheney's Metchosin farmhouse. Captain Langford, perhaps because he disliked Lewis or because he thought Mary could do better, refused to permit their marriage. In 1861 Mary returned to England with her family. Nine years later, Lewis went to London, found Mary, proposed once again and this time was accepted. The two returned to Victoria where they lived on Belleville Street until their deaths more than thirty years later.

The Governor, the Langfords and the McKenzies usually restricted their guest lists to officers. Ordinary seamen and the members of the colony's

PACIFIC FLEET, *at anchor in Esquimalt Harbour, 1867 - 1870.*

labouring class were seldom part of the festivities.

"Great Ball held at Victoria, riff-raff excluded," grumbled Robert Melrose, an indentured worker at Craigflower.[48]

Farm workers at Craigflower and the other PSAC farms amused themselves by heavy drinking. The sailors did likewise. And it was with feelings of solidarity that Melrose recorded in his diary that a sailor from the *Trincomalee* " . . . got himself hurt by falling from a tree, after drinking a bottle of Grog on top of it." An event which perhaps prompted two officers from the *Trincomalee* to hold a prayer meeting at Craigflower three weeks later.

Over the years the officers and men of the Royal Navy would add a spice to life in Victoria and while some Victorians might complain about the rowdiness of ordinary seamen, most seem to have been quite enamoured with the antics of young officers, whether it was Sub-lieutenant Sydney Smith Haldeman Dickens, the novelist's youngest son, over-acting in the theatrical performances staged by the officers of *Zealous* to entertain the citizenry or Lieutenant Horace Lascelles, the seventh son of the third Earl of Harewood, kidnapping the editor of a Victoria newspaper who had had the temerity to criticize the manner in which he conducted a punitive raid against a tribe of northern Indians. But of all the men who served on the Esquimalt Station, the most affectionately remembered was Admiral Lord Charles Beresford.

9.
"Charlie B"

The second son of the fourth Marquess of Waterford, Lord Charles Beresford, or Charlie B. as he was widely known, was a nineteen year old midshipman when he arrived at Esquimalt aboard the *Clio* in 1865. During the five months he spent on the Esquimalt Station he became a familiar figure on the rough road that ran from the naval base to Victoria.[49] His usual conveyance was a piebald pony, the only horse within the financial reach of midshipmen. But it rankled Charlie, a connoisseur of fine horseflesh and an expert rider, to be seen aboard a horse everyone knew to be rented by the hour. And so he painted the pony black. A ruse that worked well until it rained and the paint ran in rivulets off the pony and onto the street.

Charlie had the endearing quality of being able to laugh even when the joke was on him. But he did enjoy it rather more when someone else was the object of fun. One day Charlie was spotted aboard his painted pony, tearing hell-for-leather along the Esquimalt Road with a fat, flapping goose tucked under each arm and with a farmer in pursuit. Charlie disappeared around a curve in the road and when the farmer overtook him, he found his geese fluttering free and a gasping midshipman collapsed by the side of the road clutching his sides as he rocked with laughter. After Charlie caught his breath, he paid the man for his birds and then invited him to dine aboard the *Clio*.

At a time when practical jokes were thought to be the very height of wit, Charlie B. carefully followed the code of ethics by which such jokes were judged. A good practical joke should be original, unrepeatable, and harmless to everyone concerned. One afternoon Charlie, followed by a collection of midshipmen marching with un-navy-like precision, strode solemnly into the dining room of one of Victoria's best hotels. Climbing on top of a marble table, he announced that he would now hold an auction. Recognizing only bids from midshipmen and declaring an item sold before it had fetched anything like its actual cost, he auctioned off the entire contents of the hotel's larder. "I think the pig brought three shillings and a turkey sold for half a dollar," one onlooker remembered. Charlie ordered all the food collected and sent to the *Clio* where that night the midshipmen enjoyed a "glorious feast" quite unlike their usual fare which Charlie described as "our miserable rations." He returned the next day and paid the hotel's proprietor, as the man, who had calmly watched Charlie's performance, had known he would.

In December 1865 after falling into the *Clio's* hold and fracturing three ribs, Charlie Beresford sailed out of Esquimalt but he remained in the memory of many Victorians who seemed never to tire of recounting his escapades and who avidly followed his career.[50]

In 1882 as the commander of the *Condor* he played a key role in the siege of Alexandria. At great risk he sailed his little ship under the guns of a cliff-top fortress. After silencing the enemy guns, Beresford was welcomed back

HMS CLIO. *Charles Beresford served aboard* HMS Clio *on the Es-quimalt Station in 1865. A 22-gun corvette, the* Clio *was notable for her slack discipline. Her captain ran so easy-going a ship that she earn-ed the nickname* Privateer.

to the main body of the fleet with the signal "Well done, *Condor!*" The phrase became synonymous with the success of the campaign and wrapped itself gloriously around Charlie for the rest of his life.

Two years later he took part in the Nile Expedition to relieve General Gordon under the siege at Khartoum. He was mentioned in despatches as an officer "whose ability as a leader is equalled only by his daring." The London *Times* opined that nothing had "impressed the public imagination more deeply than his keeping the *Sophia* under heavy fire, which he steadily return-ed, while his engineer repaired the boiler." Had Charlie been concerned about the danger? Well, he allowed, "It *would* have been hard to die without know-ing who had won the Derby."

Even as his fame and responsibilities grew, Charlie B. remained addicted to foolish fun. He was prepared to go to almost any lengths to win a bet. He would, he declared, walk naked from Hyde Park to his club in St. James Street. Disbelievers, who had wagered considerable sums in the conviction that no Junior Naval Lord would dare do any such thing, gathered at the appointed hour. Charlie appeared — stark naked as promised — strolling unconcernedly along inside a slowly drawn carriage from which the floor boards had been removed.

His irrepressible high spirits, his ability to make people laugh and his status as the second son of the Marquess of Waterford led him inexorably into the Marlborough House set, the collection of witty, ambitious, high-born sophisticates who became the chosen friends of the Prince of Wales. Charlie, a man's man who sneered at the "sycophantic servility" of others who were close to the Prince, became Bertie's "great and very old friend." Only Charlie Beresford would have dared to send the telegram which quickly became a legend. Invited by Bertie to dine at Marlborough House, Charlie wired back,

"Regret cannot come. Lie follows by post."

He was her "Little Rascal," Princess Alexandra declared and even Queen Victoria admitted that she found Lord Charles "very funny."

His effect on lesser women was quite devastating. The combination of good looks, good humour and an unwavering roguishness was well nigh irresistible. "I enjoy making women cry," Charlie mused. "It's such fun to hear their stays creak."

But he was far from ungallant. Elizabeth Fisher had met Charlie at Esquimalt in 1865 when she was seventeen. In 1896 she was introduced to him in London as Mrs. Charles Pooley. Without missing a beat Charlie exclaimed, "Why, it's Lizzie Fisher. It must be months since we met."

"It was all of thirty years," Lizzie sighed.

At week-end house parties, Charlie remained alert to the slightly raised eyebrow, the knowing look which suggested that he would be welcome later that night in a lady's bedroom. His chief problem was locating the right door along the dimly lit hallways of sprawling country houses. On one occasion he stole into a darkened room and with a triumphant cry of "Cock-a-doodle-do" leapt onto the bed. And found himself astride a considerably shaken Bishop of Chester.

A woman caused the only serious rift between Charlie and the Prince. She was the beautiful Lady Brooke, known as Daisy to her friends and as "Babbling Brook" to journalists. Daisy had found herself married to a man who rather unchivalrously declared, "A good days' fishing and hunting is second in point of pleasure to nothing on earth." As members of the Marlborough House set, she and her husband were often in the company of Lord Charles and his wife, Mina, and Daisy began to send her unmistakable signals to the dashing naval hero whenever he hove into view.

In the late 1880's they became lovers, both of them intending their liaison to be nothing more than an amusing dalliance. But Daisy, having experienced Lord Charles, could be content with nothing less. One night she strode into Lady Charles' bedroom and told her that she and Charlie had become lovers and that Mina would have to resign herself to giving him up. Mina acted promptly, packing Charlie up and taking him home with her. And there it might have ended, for the navy soon sent Charlie out of harm's way. But it soon became apparent that Mina was pregnant. Daisy was infuriated. How dare he make love to his wife! She wrote him a scalding letter telling him what she thought of his infidelity — a letter which Mina intercepted and which contained the interesting news that one of Daisy's children was Charlie's.

Daisy would discover that she had seriously misjudged the depth of affection that existed between Mina and Charlie. On the surface, Mina seemed an odd choice for a man like Lord Charles. She was several years older than her husband and she seems to have been quite hairless — a lack she corrected by wearing wigs, false eyelashes and false eyebrows. To further enhance her appearance she wore heavy make-up causing much comment at a time when rouge was worn only by actresses and courtesans. "Here comes my freshly painted little cutter," Charlie once remarked when she entered a room. But Mina possessed qualities that Charlie much admired, not the least of which was an unflappable equanimity in the face of danger. On one occasion she and Charlie were aboard a ship which was accidentally rammed. The captain, Charlie explained, would try to beach the ship before it sank. But if that proved impossible, he would throw Mina overboard and jump in after her. Mina, who couldn't swim, looked steadily at Charlie. "That," she said, "will be very disagreeable."

LADY BROOKE. *"From the beginning of our life together my husband seemed to accept the inevitability of my having a train of admirers,"* Daisy stated matter-of-factly. Queen Victoria found her, "Very fast — very fast."

In writing to Charlie, Daisy had inadvertently delivered to Mina an instrument of blackmail. Mina deposited the letter with her solicitor and informed Daisy that she would make its contents public if she made any further attempts to lure her husband away.

Daisy, appreciating the problems she had created for herself called on the Prince. Since he was a friend of all concerned parties, would he, Daisy coaxed, use his influence to get her letter back? The Prince, ever sensitive to the problems of wildly attractive matrons in distress, agreed to do what he could. He called on Mina's solicitor and browbeat him into showing him the letter. "The most shocking letter I have ever read," Bertie said. He called on Lady Charles. Unless she returned the letter, Bertie threatened, she and Charlie would no longer be invited to Marlborough House. Reeling with righteous indignation, Mina refused. When Beresford learned of Bertie's interference he called on the Prince and accused him of behaving "like a blackguard and a coward." Finally he gave the heir to the throne an exasperated shove and Bertie stumbled backward into a chair murmuring, "Really, Lord Charles. You forget yourself."

Daisy became one of the Prince's "favourites." And Beresford, banned from the Prince's society and no longer diverted by the distractions of Marlborough House, concentrated on his naval career. In 1911, when he returned briefly to Victoria to lecture its citizens on their Imperial Responsibilities, he came as a recently retired admiral and Commander-in-Chief of the Channel Fleet.

ADMIRAL LORD CHARLES BERESFORD, *Commander of the Channel Fleet, 1907. Winston Churchill was not among Beresford's admirers. He described Charlie B. as "one of those orators of whom it is said that before they get up to speak they do not know what they are going to say, when they are speaking they do not know what they are saying, and when they have sat down they do not know what they have said."*

"A tornado of . . . enthusiasm" greeted Beresford when he rose to address the members of the Canadian Club. His listeners hung on every word and calls of "Hear, hear" and outbursts of applause punctuated his speech.[51] But his reception might have been even more tumultuous had his audience known that the sixty-five year old man, the great man some remembered as a "larky" midshipman, who stood before them carried on his back a fading tattoo of the Waterford fox-hounds, racing at full cry down from his shoulders, in pursuit of a fox whose tail could be seen disappearing between his buttocks.

II. The Gold Rush

1.
"dollars, dollars, dollars!"

Rumours that gold was to be found on the bars of the Fraser River had reached Fort Victoria as early as 1856. The following year Douglas had taken delivery of a soda-water bottle half full of gold collected by the Indians along the North Thompson. The Governor recognized the importance of the gold discoveries. Victoria, he predicted, would become a "great city." Dismissing Douglas' prediction as nothing more than an attempt to inflate the price of Company-owned town lots, residents of the colony were unprepared when they found themselves in the middle of a gold rush.

On Sunday morning April 25, 1858 parishioners were emerging from the Victoria District Church which stood on the high ground within the Church Reserve when they spotted the *Commodore*, a wooden side-wheel American steamer, entering the harbour. She carried 450 Fraser-bound miners who, when they disembarked, more than doubled the population of the town.

News that there was gold to be found on the mainland had reached San Francisco and there, just a short steamer-voyage away, were thousands of men who had gained valuable experience along California's "Trail of '49" and who planned to put their experience to use in this new, northern gold rush. Between 10,000 and 20,000 people streamed into Victoria during the last seven months of 1858. Many only paused on their way to the mainland but some chose to remain at Victoria to speculate on land or to open businesses.

The little town was swamped by this flood of humanity. Having no hotels, Victoria was soon surrounded by a sea of grey canvas tents. It became a transient city populated, some felt, by the "outscourings" of the jails of California. Many of them had arrived with no more property than the cloth-wrapped bundles they carried with them. But "dollars, dollars, dollars!" was "stamped on every face."[1]

"Victoria," one observer noted, "was assailed by an indescribable array of Polish Jews, Italian fishermen, French cooks, jobbers, speculators of every kind, land agents, auctioneers, bummers, bankrupts, and brokers of every description."[2]

Residents of the colony, after recovering from their astonishment at the magnitude and character of this invasion, became caught up in speculation-fever. Some cashed in quickly. One man who had purchased a horse in the morning for $100, sold it later that same day for $150 and considered himself a shrewd investor. Some who had the good fortune to own houses in town, rented them out for as much as $100 a month and removed to the countryside to count their money. Others sold their town lots for what they believed to be a peak price and put on the airs they thought appropriate for persons who had all the money they could ever need. Some, swept away by the rapid growth they were witnessing, concluded that the town would sprawl over the lower Island and bought large blocks of rural property which would wait for some fifty years before becoming urban and valuable. But some with an eye to the main chance made solid fortunes.

James Yates, born in Scotland in 1819, had signed on with the HBC as a ships' carpenter in 1849. Assigned to Fort Victoria, Yates balked at the Company's rigid, military-like discipline and soon earned a reputation as a "cantankerous being". Eighteen months after he arrived at the fort, he had a serious falling out with Company management. Leaving his wife behind, Yates deserted the Company service and ran off to California. While Mrs. Yates, an "active agreeable pleasant little woman with auburn hair," took in washing, worked as a seamstress and was finally forced to sell her clothes to support herself, her husband tested his luck in the California goldfields. When he returned for his wife, Yates was discovered by a Company officer and thrown into the north-east bastion where he was imprisoned for a month.

JAMES YATES AND HIS WIFE. With Amelia Douglas acting as midwife, Mrs. Yates gave birth to two children at Fort Victoria. Amelia insisted that she kneel down beside the bed which, Mrs. Yates reported, did her "a great deal of good."

Adamantly refusing to work for the Company when he emerged from jail, Yates was allowed to assume independent status. He purchased some of the first town lots sold by the HBC and in 1851 built his house and business premises outside the pickets of the fort. Yates who described himself as a wine and spirit merchant, was supplying a commodity much in demand when the gold rush deposited thousands of customers on his doorstep. Using the profits from his saloon, he covered his land holdings, which included all the town lots between Langley and Wharf Streets, with substantial brick and stone buildings from which he received an income of $1000 a month. By 1860 he was believed to be the wealthiest man in Victoria. The Yates endeared themselves to those less fortunate by refusing to let their riches go to their heads. "Neither Mr. or Mrs. Yates has got any nasty pride," one admirer reported.[3]

The HBC, which owned all the land other than the small area north of the fort which had been in the hands of private owners when the gold rush began, reacted as if emerging from a corporate fog. The Company began by asking $50 for a 60x120 foot lot, the price that had been in effect since sales had begun seven or eight years earlier. Gradually they increased the price to $100, only to find that weeks later the same property, sold and resold, would fetch $3000.

YATES STREET, *during the gold rush. On Yates Street near Government, hurriedly-built wooden shanties served as hotels. For a dollar a night, a miner was given one of the cots ranged together under low attic roofs. Required to provide their own bedding, miners packed around blankets — usually dark blue, the colour least likely to show the dirt.*

"Shops, stores and wooden shanties of every description, and in every direction, were now seen going up, and nothing was to be heard but the stroke of the chisel and hammer," an observer noted.[4] In six weeks, during the summer of 1858, 225 buildings, nearly 200 of them shops and stores had been built. Annie Deans who had been in the colony since 1853 recorded her amazement at the scene.[5] "In the morning there will be bonny green grass, at night there be a house on it." They were, Annie reported, building in the fields where carrots and turnips grew, a fact that might account for the scarcity of vegetables that summer.

The fort's bakery, located in a whitewashed log building just outside the eastern gate, had difficulty meeting the demand and when the baker ran out of flour, the populace was reduced to eating ships' biscuits and hardtack.

Prices of all commodities rose to reflect the demand. By the summer of 1858, bread was selling for twenty-five cents a loaf, butter was fetching one dollar per pound and a pound of tea cost an "outrageous" twenty-five cents.

A summer-supply of fresh, sweet water had been a problem since the establishment of the fort. A well within the fort enclosure had provided only an intermittent supply and the water from the well near the head of James Bay was of "indifferent quality." When the water became so foul as to be undrinkable, schoolboys were dispatched in a canoe to collect water from the stream that flowed into Rock Bay. None of these sources could begin to meet the demand in 1858 but entrepreneurial initiative rose to the occasion by providing fresh water at three dollars per barrel, a price that was considered exorbitant although workmen's wages had risen to the dizzying heights of ten to fifteen dollars a day.

Miners were attracted to the fort's well, the water in which, while it was difficult to get, had the advantage of being free. The well dropped straight for thirty feet, then hit bedrock and glanced off at an angle toward the harbour. During the summer the upper part of the well would become dry, but some three to four feet of water might remain in the lower part. On one occasion a miner was hauling up a kettleful of water when the rope broke. Wanting to get his kettle back, he paid an Indian to retrieve it for him. The Indian stood on the dry part of the well and tried unsuccessfully to reach the kettle. Deciding to help him, the miner swung himself down on a rope. When he had descended some ten feet his foot struck the rocks which lined the well and without warning the entire rock wall collapsed, crushing the Indian and killing him instantly.[6] After his body was recovered, the well was ordered to be completely filled in and was forgotten until it was rediscovered over one hundred years later during renovations to the building which had been built on top of it. (*site 16*)

WINDSOR HOTEL. *Built in 1858, the Windsor was the first brick hotel to appear in the city. The oldest brick building in British Columbia, it survives today, its graceful arches displaced by plate glass display windows and its bricks overlaid with neo-Tudor half-timbering.*

Ship-owners in San Francisco maximized their profits by advertising cut-rate fares and then overcrowding their vessels. Most steamers outbound from San Francisco anchored at Esquimalt which had a deeper and more easily entered harbour than Victoria. Before the gold rush began, travellers along the trail that connected Esquimalt and Victoria "used to flounder through the mud without meeting a single soul." But by the summer of 1858 it was "covered with pedestrians toiling along, crowded with well-laden carts and and vans . . . and with strangers of every tongue and country." And, it should be noted, the Esquimalt road had become the scene of "diabolical spectacles" capable of shocking to the core a respectable itinerant Fellow of the Royal Geographical Society.[7]

Matthew Macfie arrived in Victoria in September 1859 a year after the rush had reached its peak. Macfie calculated that the town had a permanent population of fifteen hundred which would soon be swelled by over-wintering miners who often remained in town until the level of mainland rivers dropped in late spring. While he dutifully made notes about the geology and topography of the place, Macfie, like other newcomers, found himself fascinated by the Songhees and their village.

"I have witnessed scenes after sunset calculated to shock even the bluntest sensibilities," Macfie wrote with the air of a man preparing to exploit vice by publicly deploring it. The fires in the village cast a "lurid glare" upon the waters, he continued. To the town came the sounds of "loud and discordant whoopings" from natives "infuriated with bad liquor." But it took more than a few noisy drunks to horrify Macfie. What he found appalling and "a scandal to the country" was Indian prostitution.

The Songhees village was located beside the Esquimalt road, easily accessible to the hordes of unattached young men who made Victoria their temporary home. Douglas and other Company men who had witnessed the strangely exaggerated effect that alcohol had on the natives had taken care to limit its availability, but now saloons abounded "vastly out of proportion to the wants of the population" and spirits were easily available provided one had the price of a drink. To raise the money to buy liquor, Indian men became procurers, selling the favours of Indian women from other tribes who had been taken in battle and who, as prisoners-of-war, became their captors' slaves.

"One cannot walk up the Esquimalt road by day or night without encountering the sight of these Indian slaves squatting in considerable numbers in the bush," Macfie noted, adding that their purpose was not difficult to imagine. Particularly discerning were the men of the Royal Navy. "The extent to which the nefarious practices are encouraged by the crews of Her Majesty's ships is a disgrace to the service they represent," Macfie chided.

If the customer didn't come to them, some Indians chose to become door-to-door salesmen. "So unblushingly is this traffic carried on, that I have seen the husband and wife of a native family canvassing from one miner's shanty to another, with the view of making assignations for the squaws in their possession," Macfie gasped.

Indian drunkenness and prostitution were to play key roles in a public drama played out a few years later.

2.
"judicial murder"

Allache was a young Tsimshian who, in 1858, had come to Victoria with his wife. He was not unfamiliar with the pleasures of alcohol, but no evidence would suggest that he was an habitual drunkard or a brawler. Thomas Brown, a black American miner, unable to recognize the difference between a slave-prostitute and a respectable married woman, was attracted to Allache's wife. Allache, who couldn't speak English, had protested as forcefully as he could when Brown began to visit their tent. In spite of Allache's repeated warnings, the man returned again and again and Allache was forced to witness daily assaults on his wife.

Finally he was able to stand it no longer. "Half maddened by drink," he fell upon Brown and stabbed him. A few days later Brown died and Allache was arrested and charged with murder.

He stood trial for his life, undefended and supplied with an Indian interpreter whose familiarity with English was poor and whose knowledge of the Tsimshian dialect was non-existent. "A lonely, helpless victim," Allache was found guilty and sentenced to hang. Attempts were made to have him pardoned but the pardon was denied. It was important to set an example. Indians must be taught to respect the law.

At eight o'clock on the morning of Saturday, August 25, 1860 a crowd of some three hundred Victorians had gathered around a scaffold erected in the yard beside the Police Barracks, a multi-purpose building constructed in 1859 which served as police headquarters, the jail and the courthouse and would soon function as City Hall. Allache, "his eyes streaming with tears," was brought to the foot of the scaffold. As the rope was placed around his neck, he filled his lungs and throwing back his head, he breathed forth one long, loud, lamentable wail. A thrill of horror jolted through the crowd and men began to cry. Half the spectators hurried away, unable to endure the sight any longer.[8]

After dangling from the rope for an hour, Allache was cut down. Placed in a black coffin, he was buried in the barracks-yard, where his bones may yet lie under the paving of Bastion Square. (*site 17*)

To Alfred Waddington, Allache's hanging was "judicial murder" and at his own expense he published a pamphlet condemning the "mockery of a trial" that had led to his conviction.[9] A champion of unpopular causes, Waddington was something of an oddity in gold rush Victoria. He was older and better educated than most other residents of the town, but what really set him apart was his liberalism and his possession of a genuinely compassionate conscience.

Waddington was born near London in 1801. Educated in Paris and at German universities, he had worked in France before travelling to California. By the 1850's he was a partner in Dulip & Waddington, a wholesale grocery firm in San Francisco. Waddington came to Victoria in the spring in 1858 to open a branch of his San Francisco business. As one of the first to arrive on the scene, he was able to buy a key piece of property between Johnson and Yates Streets. He cut an alley through his property, giving him six hundred feet of street frontage. (*site 25*) Dividing the land along Waddington Alley into small lots, he erected buildings of redwood he had imported from California and leased them out to a variety of tenants, including a fish market, a bakery, a blacksmith, the Sacramento Restaurant and the Bowling and Refreshment Saloon.

POLICE BARRACKS, *Bastion Square. Public hangings took place in the yard beside the Police Barracks, the large castellated building on the right. The false-fronted wooden building on the left is the Boomerang Inn which provided a convivial atmosphere for the juries sent there to consider their verdicts.*

Waddington became a tireless critic of the colonial administration. He called public meetings. He wrote letters-to-the-editor. He produced pamphlets which he paid for and distributed himself. Whatever the specific issue, Waddington's main theme remained the same. The Company men and the appointed officials who made up the ruling class and who, together with the officers of the Royal Navy, continued to form the colony's social elite, were adopting policies which were advantageous to themselves rather than beneficial to the colony as a whole.

Money had been spent to lay out the townsite, to fill in the ravine, to improve streets and to build bridges. Improvements which, Waddington asserted, benefited only land speculators. The miners, the men who had brought prosperity to the colony, were isolated at their diggings with no wagon roads, no food, no provisions and no postal service. Meanwhile, balls and other entertainments costing as much as $1,600 had been organized to amuse visiting naval officers.

Although prepared to drive himself to exhaustion in pursuit of his goals, Waddington was not a particularly effective campaigner. A bit of a fussbudget, he was easily dismissed as "Old Waddy" and seldom taken seriously by the younger men who held positions of power.

His chief opponent was George Hunter Cary, the Attorney-General. Thirty years younger than Waddington, Cary had arrived in Victoria in 1859 armed with "six law books, a carpetbag and a toothbrush." Never the most stable of men, Cary's erratic and excitable temperament occasionally got him in trouble with the law for riding his horse through town at breakneck speed and along pedestrian footpaths. Cary, who would slip quickly into insanity and die in 1866 of "an overworked brain and a weak constitution," seems to have taken particular pleasure in goading Waddington to the point of apoplexy after the older man won election to the assembly in 1860.

"The attorney-general was ill and irritable, Mr. Waddington was old and irritable," the speaker of the house recalled. "The manner in which those two would hammer away at each other was most refreshing to outsiders who gathered at the hall."[10]

GEORGE HUNTER CARY AND HIS WIFE. *The Attorney-General of the Colony of Vancouver Island, Cary was described in 1861 as, "Shallow beyond belief; conceited beyond conception; untruthful and unscrupulous," and "devoid of correct governing principles." Aside from that, and his tendency to drink too much and ride too fast, there was nothing very much wrong with him.*

Unlike the Attorney-General, Waddington was something of a visionary. Waddington, who campaigned for Victoria's incorporation, was convinced that the town would become an important city — but only if the Island and British Columbia were linked by a railroad to the Canadian provinces to the east. In 1867 Waddington travelled to Ottawa — a long journey for an ailing old man which took him down the west coast, across Panama, and up the east coast to New York. After presenting his arguments in favour of a transcontinental rail line, he journeyed to London where he hoped to interest British financiers in the idea. He returned to Ottawa and although he was suffering dreadfully from gout and was often confined to bed, he continued to argue fervently for the railroad. "Old Waddy" had no way of knowing that the Prime Minister considered him nothing more than "a respectable old fool."

In February 1872, Waddington was staying in Ottawa waiting to witness the passage of the railway bill. He had spent an uneasy few months. Smallpox had been "quite epidemic" in Ottawa that winter and Waddington had a particular dread of the disease. One February afternoon, he was standing in the lobby of his hotel and talking, as always, about his railway scheme to a group of potential investors. An acquaintance, an Ottawa doctor, delighted to happen upon Waddington, approached him, clasped his hands warmly and, in response to a polite enquiry from Waddington, said, "I have just left the worst case of confluent small pox I have ever seen."[11]

Waddington snatched back his hands and trembling violently stumbled to a chair. He died on February 27, 1872 — of smallpox.

ALFRED WADDINGTON. *Waddington's Fraser Mines Vindicated was the first book written and published in British Columbia.*

3
"choked with putrescent filth"

Like any boom-town, Victoria suffered from the effects of rapid, unplanned growth.

Some of the streets which had been traced on the early plans of the townsite were sold and built upon, forcing land owners to cut alleyways through their properties if they wished to have street access. (*site 21*)

During dry summer months, swirling dust choked Victoria's streets and water was in such short supply that little could be spared for sprinkling the roadways. If the evidence of one observer is to be believed, it might have been more practical to dampen the dust with HBC rum.

"Liquor was cheaper than water," he recalled. "We remember on a hot day in July seeing a perspiring man enter a saloon on Yates street to ask for a glass of water. 'Water!' gasped the astonished barkeeper. 'Why, stranger, I'll *give* you a glass of rum but two bits is the price of water at this yere [sic] bar'."[12]

In winter, the situation was reversed. "In the town of Victoria the mud is so deep that it comes up to the horses' girths & foot passengers can only cross on planks laid across," one visitor recorded.[13] The mud-filled streets produced legends all their own, the most common being the story of a merchant who, wanting to carry on a conversation with a friend on the other side of the street, hired an Indian with a bow and arrow to shoot letters across the quagmire.

YATES STREET, *looking west from Government. The state of the streets was "simply indescribable, mud without end . . . occasional placards informed the public that no bottom was to be found."*

In any season, the lack of a sewage system brought its own kind of urban blight. Outhouses and privies were sited for their users' convenience with little thought given to property lines or neighbourly esthetics. Running into the street in soapy streams was the effluvium from public bath houses. Cesspools often overflowed into the drainage ditches which lined the streets.

"The gutters in the main streets are at times choked with putrescent filth," the *British Colonist*, one of Victoria's earliest newspapers, reported in 1861.[14]

With barnyard animals confined in small city pens and horses providing the only means of transportation and housed in stables throughout the business district, more than dust must have risen on the summer wind to delight sensitive nostrils.

Sensibilities of a different kind were outraged by the behaviour of prostitutes who had left the Esquimalt road and moved into town. No longer Indian-controlled, the trade had been organized by men, both black and white, who collected their squaws into brothels, in the shanties along Kanaka road.

"Hardly a day passes without fights between squaws and squawmen," the *Colonist* fumed. "Yesterday morning we observed two squaws fighting in the middle of the street and they could not be induced to desist until one had nearly denuded the other of her clothing."[15]

Pressured to solve the problem of the brothels, the colonial legislature decided to adopt a pragmatic approach. Businesses in the city depended on the miners who came to town for the winter and who soon became bored with nothing to do.

"They wander around and through the town in quest of a little excitement and naturally bop into every hole and corner whence a little fun is to be had," one of their number reported.[16]

If some form of amusement was not provided, the men might choose to overwinter elsewhere and it was an undeniable fact that many miners found their amusements along Kanaka road. So rather than abolish bawdy houses, the legislature chose instead to license them as "dance halls."

The euphemism fooled no one, least of all Amor de Cosmos, bachelor-editor of the *Colonist*. "They are sinks of iniquity and pollution," he thundered. "Prostitution and kindred vices, in all their hideous deformity, and disease in every form, lurk there."[17] And while less-fevered minds suggested that since it was impossible to prevent prostitution, it might be better to have a few sinks of iniquity rather than having the whole town turn into a cesspool, De Cosmos and the petitioners who insisted that the dance halls be closed represented a popular point of view.

While prostitution was a nuisance and foul smelling drains and ditches were an annoyance and a potential health hazard, the possibility of a major fire was an ever-present threat. With its straw-filled stables and with its hotels, saloons and dance halls lit by candles or gas lamps and heated by woodstoves, Victoria, like any wood-built town was particularly vulnerable to fire. Compounding the problem was the greediness of property-owners who covered every square inch of their town lots with buildings — a practice which denied

FORT STREET, *looking east from Government. Fort Street extended only as far as Douglas Street. Planks bridged open gutters and crossed the street at intersections.*

51

fire-fighters access to the rear and sides of buildings and increased the likelihood of a fire in one spreading to its neighbours.

As early as 1858 Douglas had ordered fire-fighting equipment from San Francisco and in April of the following year the chain gang from the city jail had been ordered to build two cisterns, one on Store Street and the other on Government Street, each containing some 25,000 gallons of water. Recognizing these steps as a precaution, but not a solution, Douglas adopted other measures to ensure the safety of government buildings.

The Police Barracks built in 1859 hard by the northern palisade of the fort, was constructed of brick and deemed to be "fire-proof." The 'Bird-cages,' the buildings that would house all departments of the growing colonial government, were sited away from the city across the harbour on the banks of James Bay on land adjacent to Douglas' holdings and safely removed from any civic holocaust.

JAMES BAY BRIDGE AND THE 'BIRDCAGES'. *A bridge connected the James Bay district with the city until 1901 when the James Bay mud flats were filled in and a causeway was built.*

Christened the 'Birdcages,' perhaps because their appearance reminded some of the ornamental birdcages popular at the time and perhaps because the road that separated the legislative precinct from Douglas' land had been named Birdcage Walk after the London street of the same name which runs from Buckingham Palace to the Houses of Parliament, the colonial buildings were designed by Berlin-born architect and civil engineer Hermann Otto Tiedemann, who had a particular talent for producing buildings which defied apt comparisons. (*site 17*)

The central or Administrative Building, ". . . resembles in its mixed style of architecture, the latest fashion of Chinese pagoda, Swiss cottage and Italian villa," one observer noted, and then, having given the matter more thought, decided that the architectural style was "Elizabethan."[18] More like a "Dutch Toy," others grumbled.

As the problems in the town increased, so did the pressure on the colonial legislature to pass an act of incorporation which would allow Victorians to raise money for civic improvements and to enact by-laws controlling development. The Act of Incorporation was passed on August 2, 1862 and two weeks later the first elections were held.

4.
"our Falstaffian mayor"

Eligible voters, who included only British subjects who were male and who owned or leased property valued at £20 or more, gathered in the Barracks-yard to elect, by a show of hands, Victoria's first mayor. There were two candidates for office: Alfred Waddington and Thomas Harris. While Waddington received only four votes, Harris was supported by a "forest of hands." The results surprised no one. Waddington was regarded as the self-appointed conscience of the city; Harris was the very model of a small town mayor.

Born in Hertfordshire in 1817 and the son of a farmer, Harris had gone to California in 1853. Like so many others, he had seen the British Columbia gold rush as an opportunity to make the most of experience he had gained in California. He arrived in Victoria in 1858 and opened the Queen's Market, the town's first butcher shop. A three hundred pound giant of a man, he was renowned for his joviality and generosity. That he was a well-known sportsman only increased his electability.

QUEEN'S MARKET. *Harris, who campaigned for office as an 'umble tradesman, operated the Queen's Market, Victoria's first butcher shop. Harris began his business by buying two sheep from the HBC and selling mutton retail from a tent.*

Rather too heavy to play in the cricket games which were staged at Beacon Hill Park, Harris excelled at horse racing. A rough race-course encircling Beacon Hill had been developed several years before the 179 acres had been set aside as a park reserve in 1858. And there Harris was a well-known figure, thundering around the mile-long course. His two chief opponents were Lieutenant Commander the Hon. Horace Douglas Lascelles and innkeeper John

Howard. "These three were inseparables, especially when horse races were in question," a fellow enthusiast recalled.[19] And it is unlikely that anywhere but Victoria so disparate a threesome could have come together as friends to encourage the development of the sport of kings.

Appearing vaguely effeminate despite the luxuriant sideburns which curled over his jaw and met under his chin, Lascelles was the seventh son of the third Earl of Harewood. He had joined the Royal Navy in 1848 when he was thirteen and from 1862-1865 he served on the Esquimalt Station as the commander of the gun-boat *Forward*. Possessed of "an amiability of disposition which endeared him to all who knew him," Lascelles was regarded as a kind and generous man. And it was presumed that both kindness and generosity had prompted him to establish a little house on the Esquimalt road in which lived several young Englishmen who had gone broke looking for gold. Lascelles was well-liked in Victoria, partly because he was a lavish spender and partly because he "never made any virtuous pretensions, nor posed as a moral man."[20]

HON. HORACE DOUGLAS LAS-CELLES, *on the right. Lascelles was thirty-four when he died in his little Esquimalt cottage, alone except for his tame silver fox and his golden pheasant.*

As well as spending freely, Lascelles invested heavily — in coal mines near Nanaimo and in businesses in Victoria. His investments were directed by Joseph Johnson Southgate, a former ship-master who had moved to Victoria from San Francisco in 1859 to act as a commission merchant and naval supplier and who became Lascelles' "devoted friend." (*site 14*)

The third member of the racing triumverate, John Thomas Howard was not nearly so high-born as Lascelles. Originally from Manchester, he had come to Victoria by way of California where he had grubbed together enough gold to allow him to open the Royal Oak Inn at Esquimalt. Howard was a born publican. He enjoyed swapping stories with the seamen who made their way to his harbour-side establishment. He revelled in the company of the "fighting men, sharpers and that sort" who bellied up to his bar and who were as anxious as he to find something — anything — on which to make a wager. A scrappy little man, he was prepared to draw himself up to his full five and a half feet to match his dog, his cricket bat, his fists and his horses with anyone. He imported Kentucky-bred horses for his racing stable and if the bloodlines of his horses and his own skill as a jockey were not enough to guarantee victory, he was quite prepared to cheat and to fall upon any man who suggested he was less than honest.

VICTORIA CRICKET ELEVEN, *c. 1860. John Howard, standing second from right. Howard, always looking for something on which to make a wager, took space in the newspaper to announce that he was the best cricketeer in the country and to issue a $1000 challenge to anyone who might care to prove otherwise.*

Harris, Howard and Lascelles — the "Falstaffian" butcher, the diminutive innkeeper and the effete naval officer — were "kindred spirits" providing many a day's sport for the citizens of Victoria, who enjoyed witnessing the tactics adopted to insure victory as much as they enjoyed the races. With Harris' horse wheezing under his three hundred pound bulk, it was necessary to provide some form of handicapping to make the contest equal. During the races staged in 1864 to celebrate the Queen's May 24th birthday, Lascelles and Harris were the chief opponents. Lascelles, it was decided, would carry a second rider and together they would match the mayor's weight. Harris led from the beginning and Lascelles, seeing the mayor disappear in a cloud of dust, unceremoniously jettisoned his extra cargo. But too late to prevent Harris' galloping to victory.

On August 25, 1862 Mayor Harris and the six councilmen elected to serve with him, convened the first council meeting which was held in a court room in the Police Barracks since no provisions had been made for a separate City Hall. One of the first items of business was the appointment of a "Committee of Nuisances" which would guide the council in deciding which of the many nuisances should be dealt with first.

On Yates Street the committee couldn't help but notice the "very disagreeable stench" arising from the stagnant water which had reached the street by way of the drains attached to the Colonial Hotel and the Gypsy

House Baths. The pigs which were found within the area bounded by Government, Wharf, Johnson and Yates Street, were, the committee reported, a "great nuisance" and an annoyance to the residents of those streets. In addition to the notorious dance halls, bawdy houses continued to exist. Near the gully between Johnson and Cormorant Streets, the committee discovered "a number of houses of ill fame" which were a "disgrace to the neighbourhood." The Humboldt Street brothels continued to operate. "The neighbours complain of habitual drunkenness and disgusting language being continually made use of," the committee reported.[21]

THOMAS HARRIS. *Harris proved himself more than capable of occupying the mayor's chair. At the first council meeting, as Harris lowered his bulk into the seat of office, there came a loud crash. The mayoral chair resembled a cracked eggshell. Harris had, the newspaper gleefully reported, "alighted on the floor on that portion of his breeches which wears out first."*

5.
"an abominable botch"

The first City Ordinances suggest that the council counted the "pollution" of the dance-halls and brothels as only a minor civic nuisance and concentrated on cleaning up the town physically rather than morally.

Among the thirteen by-laws passed on September 23, 1862 were several formed to prevent the town from being buried in filth or from floating away on a sea of dirty water.[22]

> * No person shall sink any privy, vault, or cesspool nearer than two feet from his neighbour's premises and not less than twenty feet from the street.

> * No person shall throw or deposit on any of the footpaths, side-walks, highways, thoroughfares, or any public place within the city limits, any rubbish, filth, ashes or offal of any kind.

Another by-law was so tortuously worded that its precise intention was not immediately apparent.

* Every person who in any thoroughfare shall beat or shake any carpet, rug, or mat, except door-mats, after the hour of eight in the morning, or throw or lay any dirt, litter, or ashes, or any carrion, fish, offal or rubbish, or throw or cause any such thing to go into any sewer pipe, or drain, or into any well, stream or water-course, or put the same in such as position that it may run into the harbour, or any pond or reservoir for water; or cause any offensive matter to run from any manufactory, brewery, slaughter-house, butcher's shop, or dung hill, or any uncovered place, whether or not surrounded by a wall or fence.

* Every person who shall empty or begin to empty any privy within the hours of 6 in the morning and 12 at night, and who shall move along any night-soil, soap-lees, ammoniacal liquor, or other such offensive matter, between the hours of six in the morning and eight in the evening, and who shall at any time use for such purpose any cart or carriage not having a proper covering, or who shall wilfully or carelessly slop or spill any such offensive matter in the removal thereof, or who shall not carefully sweep or clean away any such place in which any such offensive matter shall have been placed, spilled or slopped; and in the default of the apprehension of the actual offender, the owner of the cart or carriage employed for any such purpose shall be deemed to be the offender.

Other, more grammatically precise by-laws set the speed limit at eight miles per hour, prohibited the operation of slaughter houses, tanneries or distilleries within the city limits and provided for a fine of one pound for those found carrying loaded fire-arms or other dangerous weapons.

Proving that the colonial legislature was equally capable of drafting incomprehensible legislation, it was discovered that the attorney-general had made "an abominable botch of incorporating the city" and that the confused wording of the Act of Incorporation resulted in the city council lacking the authority to raise money by levying municipal taxation. Until the situation was clarified, the council was unable to proceed with civic improvements. However private initiative solved two of the city's more pressing problems: the shortage of water and the crime-encouraging blackness of night-time streets.

A spring, or artesian well, had been discovered in the Spring Ridge area, some two miles from town. The water was transported to the city in barrels attached to two-wheeled carts which then travelled from door to door and topped up the oak casks in which householders and businessmen stored their private supply.

In 1864 the Spring Ridge Water Company was formed and permission was sought to dig up city streets for the laying of water pipes. Running down Pandora to Government and along Government Street to the business district, the pipes — bark covered logs hollowed out and laid end to end — carried water by gravity to large standpipes which were installed at several downtown locations. Water carts could now fill their barrels at these pumps, rather than making the four mile round trip to the spring. Victorians continued to rely on Spring Ridge for their water supply until 1875 when water piped from Elk Lake began to arrive in town.

GOVERNMENT STREET, *looking north from Fort Street. A water cart is filling its barrel at the standpipe in front of the Brown Jug Saloon, the building on the far right.*

The Victoria Gas Company had been incorporated in November, 1860 making it almost two years older than the town. Originally the company had intended to deliver the gas, manufactured at its plant near Rock Bay, to "the house, shop, establishment or residence" of any person who should request the service. On September 29, 1862 gas flowed through the pipes for the first time, lighting the lantern hanging from Carroll's liquor store on Yates Street and within a week the *Colonist* was able to report that several stores and saloons were being lit by gas.[23] Some other businessmen followed Carroll's example and installed gas lanterns on the street facade of their buildings, but still Victoria's night-time streets remained very dark and more than a few accidents occurred when pedestrians who had ventured out without carrying their own lanterns stumbled on uneven planking or fell into ditches. The City was more than ready to listen to the proposal made by the Company in January, 1863. If the City agreed to buy lamps and lamp posts supplied by the Company, the Company would provide the manpower to light them and to keep them clean for a charge of $40 per month, provided that the number of lamp posts installed was fewer than fifty.[24] And soon Victoria's streets, while they were not ablaze with light, certainly were less murky than they had been before. (*site 10*) The street lighting may even have had an effect on crime, but the number of potential criminals diminished for reasons that had nothing to do with well-lit streets.

No sooner had Victorians begun to take steps to correct the problems caused by rapid growth than growth stopped. By 1864 the rush of gold-seekers who had worked their way up the Fraser River and into the Cariboo had turned into an exodus of discouraged men who had spent their savings, found no gold and, if they stopped in Victoria at all, were looking for jobs or waiting for funds from home rather than looking for places to spend their money.

WHARF STREET, *c. 1864. The 1100 block Wharf Street has changed very little since this photograph was taken during the gold rush.
On the far right, can be seen one of the Victoria Gas Company's street
lamps.*

Allen Francis, the U.S. Consul took careful note of Victoria's declining fortunes and submitted his findings in a series of reports to the American Secretary of State.[25] There had been "a great falling off of business during the last year," he reported in December, 1864. Buildings begun in the spring had been left unfinished. Property values were falling. There had been no immigration, in fact, the population had fallen by almost a thousand.

"The future prospects of the city are anything but cheering," Francis concluded. And he was quite right, for years would pass before Victoria again experienced anything like the heady days of the gold rush. And yet many might come to be thankful for the economic depression that hung over the town, for more than anything else it guaranteed that Victoria would remain British.

GOVERNMENT STREET, *east side at corner of Bastion Street. A
water cart can be seen moving up the street below one of the large
gas lamps that began lighting the city in 1864. The brick building immediately behind the lamp is the home of Thomas Harris.*

6.
"a little bit of old San Francisco"

A century later, Victoria's tourist industry would reach into the past and promote the city as a "Little Bit of Olde England." But during the 1860's Victoria could best be described as a little bit of old San Francisco.

A San Francisco based correspondent for the *Times* of London was struck by the similarity between the two cities. "I could have written a pretty correct account of the state of Victoria without going out of my office. It is the San Francisco of 1849 reproduced; and the republication of one of my letters of that period would save me the trouble of sketching the new city. The same hurry-scurry, hurly-burly, dirt, dust, inconvenience, bad living, bad housing, cheating and lying."[26]

Each fall the town's permanent population braced for the arrival of the overwintering miners, most of whom were from California, Washington or Oregon. During the winter months, Americans made up the majority of the population and although Victoria was the capital of a British colony, most of them must have felt quite at home. Businesses like the California Saloon on Johnson Street and the Sacramento Restaurant on Waddington Alley lured the American miners with familiar names and the city itself with its planked sidewalks and with its false-fronted hotels and many saloons was all but indistinguishable from other gold-built towns they might have passed through along California's "Trail of '49."

SAN FRANCISCO BATHS. *Few hotels provided facilities for washing. One of the town's many bath houses, the San Francisco attracted Americans with a familiar name.*

Before Victoria had its own foundry or brick-yard or a sawmill capable of producing finely finished lumber, building materials were imported from San Francisco and it was in San Francisco that John Wright, one of the city's first and busiest architects, had gained most of his professional experience. The city's first businesses were opened as northern branches of established San Francisco operations or by individuals who had benefited from Californian entrepreneurial experience.

So strong was American influence that the Fourth of July was celebrated with the same enthusiasm as the Queen's May 24th birthday. The American Civil War received detailed coverage in the *British Colonist* and the results of important battles were reported in special, rush editions. Americans whose sympathies differed, often fought it out on downtown streets, the most popular rioting place being the street outside the Confederate Saloon.

William Shapard, the saloon's proprietor, was southern-born. He arrived in Victoria in 1858 with his wife and children and worked as a carpenter until 1861 when he became caught up with his role as the leader of the group of men and women who formed the city's Southern colony. He rented a small brick building on Langley Street near Yates and opened the Confederate Saloon which provided him with a livelihood while it furnished a focus for his activities. In front of the saloon he erected a tall flagstaff from which he flew a Confederate flag made by the Southern ladies of Victoria. Shapard's saloon, noted for its "generous free lunches," its "excellent rye whiskey cocktails" and its all-night, high-stakes poker games, soon became infamous as a rendezvous for Southern sympathizers.[27]

The Confederate Saloon and its proprietor were anathemas to the Northerners resident in Victoria. They appealed to the American Consul, Allen Francis, suggesting that he demand the removal of the "obnoxious flag." Francis refused. Struggling to maintain his reputation among the Southerners as "an easy-going nobody," he had no interest in attracting attention to himself.

"To talk with him you would think his mind on most subjects a complete blank," recalled Canadian-born David Higgins, who as a reporter for the *Colonist* often found himself in Francis' company. "You could never apparently excite in him the slightest interest in anything concerning the plans of the Southern colony."[28]

Lulled by Francis' presumed incompetence and excited by Shapard's whiskey, the men who collected at the Confederate Saloon openly discussed plans to enter the war by outfitting privateers to prey on American shipping or by kidnapping the American Consul. Meanwhile, Francis who was "always on the alert—keen and watchful," despite appearances to the contrary, was busily preparing secret dispatches for Washington.

"Congregated here . . . are some desperate men from the rebel states talking of expeditions to California and Nevada Territory for revolutionary purposes," he reported on October 1, 1862.[29]

Unlike William Shapard who ran his sympathies up his flagpole for all to see, the proprietor of Ringo's restaurant on Yates Street chose to appear cautiously neutral. Sam Ringo was black. A former slave, he had been freed after nursing his master through an attack of smallpox. He had no interest

AMERICAN HOTEL. *Irishman Tommy Burnes, standing top-hatted in front of his hotel, chose a name which .he thought would attract the maximum number of customers. In 1893, after the wooden building burned down, Burnes rebuilt the hotel in brick on the same site on Yates Street by Commercial Alley.*

in having Civil War battles refought in his restaurant. On one occasion, Ringo heard the sounds of angry voices followed by a scuffle. He emerged from the kitchen to find the two combatants facing each other, pistols drawn. A huge man, Ringo threw his arms about the two and grappling them to his chest, he held them there until, gasping and choking, they agreed to drop their guns and shake hands.[30]

Sam Ringo was not the only American black to come to Victoria to start a new life. In 1858 a thirty-five member advance party had left San Francisco for Vancouver Island. They sent favourable reports to friends and relations in California. "All coloured man wants here is ability and money . . . It is a God-sent land for the coloured people."[31] And a few years later Victoria's black population had risen to almost 250.

7.
"a 'smart sprinkle' of blacks"

Technically slavery did not exist in California. However the *Fugitive Slave Act* permitted the arrest of any runaway slave found within the state and the *Civil Practice Act* disqualified blacks from testifying against whites. In March of 1858 an act was introduced that, had it passed, would have prevented further immigration of "negroes and mulattoes" to California and would have required the registration of all blacks already resident there.

Early in 1858, San Francisco blacks had begun to meet to discuss the possibility of emigrating. A letter of inquiry was sent to the governor of Vancouver Island. James Douglas, who was himself described as a mulatto, replied that they would find themselves welcomed in the colony. Galvanized by Douglas' assurances, thirty-five blacks booked passage aboard the *Commodore*. It wasn't until they arrived at the docks that they realized they would be sharing the ship with some four hundred Californians, some of whom were the type of men they were coming to the colony to avoid.

Some blacks succumbed to gold fever and headed for the mines. But many followed their original intention of becoming permanent settlers and taking an active part in society.

VICTORIA PIONEER RIFLES. *Formed in 1860, the 'African Rifles' was a militia corps composed entirely of forty-three blacks who had volunteered their services to protect the Colony.*

Mifflin Gibbs, free-born in Philadelphia, grumbled about the lack of initiative exhibited by the HBC. "The business portion here is generally owned by old fogies, who are destitute of Yankee enterprise," he wrote to a friend.[32] He soon provided an example of Yankee enterprise by buying a town lot and dividing the house that sat on it in two. Collecting rent from half the house, he opened Lester & Gibbs "Dealers in Groceries, Provisions, Boots, Shoes, &c." in the other. Within a few years he had become wealthy enough to hire a servant and to build a house on the five acre parcel of land he had purchased in James Bay.

Not all black men were as worthy as Mifflin Gibbs. Tom Brown had been murdered because he had repeatedly molested an Indian woman. Another black had earned public opprobrium when, losing his temper when his wagon became mired in mud, he beat his horse to death. Other black men were charged with brawling or vagrancy. The latter charge being one usually used against suspected pimps or brothel keepers. But like Gibbs and his partner Peter Lester, many of Victoria's blacks became solid citizens. Archy Lee, a former slave from Kentucky, became a porter and later a drayman. Nathan Pointer owned a clothing store on Government Street. Fortune Richard earned his living as a ships' carpenter. Wellington Moses opened the Pioneer Shaving Saloon and Bath House and by 1861 was the proprietor of a Fort Street boarding house thought sufficiently genteel to house peripatetic English gentlewomen.

Miss Sophia Cracroft travelled to Victoria with her aunt Lady Franklin, widow of the Arctic explorer. They were directed to Moses' establishment, "the very best in the place & really *very* reasonable".[33]

"It is kept by a colored man & his wife," Sophia recorded. "They are very respectable people. He is a hair cutter & has a shop — the naval people especially patronise him. His wife has the reputation of being a first rate cook."

During their stay Sophia and Lady Franklin were waited upon by prominent members of the black community, including Mifflin Gibbs, who Sophia described as "a most respectable merchant who is rising fast." They told the ladies that they had encountered prejudice in Victoria but they were convinced that it was caused by the "strong American element."

"They naturally detest America," Sophia noted with satisfaction.

When they discovered that their colour would be held against them they had contemplated leaving the colony in a body, Gibbs and his fellows informed the ladies, and they would have done so had it not been for the stand taken by the Reverend Edward Cridge.

The Anglican Dean, Cridge had arrived at Fort Victoria in 1855 to replace Robert Staines as HBC chaplain. In 1856 he officiated at the opening of Victoria's first church, the Victoria District Church on Blanshard.

REVEREND EDWARD CRIDGE. *In 1854 Cridge was engaged by the HBC to replace Robert Staines as the fort's chaplain. Before he left his West Ham parish in London's East End, he married Joseph Hitchcock and Ann Mahoney, the grandparents of Alfred Hitchcock who became famous for his direction of suspense films and infamous for his complete lack of interest in Victoria.*

As soon as Cridge learned that a party of blacks had arrived aboard the *Commodore*, he had sought them out and invited them to his church. Cridge's welcome was not extended by all members of his congregation. On August 4, 1858 a letter, from an American who used the nom de plume 'Henry Sharpstone', appeared in the *Victoria Gazette*.

"Last Sabbath was an unusually warm day," Sharpstone wrote. "The little chapel was crowded as usual with a 'smart sprinkle' of blacks, *generously* mixed with whites. The Ethiopians *perspired*! they always do when out of place. Several white gentlemen left their seats vacant, and sought the purer atmosphere outside; others moodily endured the *aromatic luxury* of their positions, in no very pious frame of mind."

The church, Sharpstone recommended, should be segregated. " . . . give the colored people a place by themselves, as is done in all respectable churches in the world . . . "

Mifflin Gibbs leapt to his own defense with an impassioned letter. He had come to Victoria, he wrote, " . . . to escape the tyranny and oppression of Republican, Democratic, church-going California."[34]

"It comes with a bad grace from Americans to talk of the horrors of amalgamation when every plantation of the South is more or less a seraglio, and numbers of the most prominent men in the State of California have manifested little heed to color in their choice of companions in an amorous intrigue or a nocturnal debauch," Gibbs continued, scoring debating points but providing information not instantly recognizable as supporting the cause of black respectability.

Cridge succeeded in taking the argument off the boil by stating that he would take note of the "expressed wishes of any individuals with regard to their own personal accommodation in the church" provided that they did not conflict with the claims of the others, but the issue of integrated seating continued to simmer until 1861 when a "race riot" broke out over theatre seating.[35]

A benefit concert, the proceeds from which were to be used to improve hospital facilities, had been planned for the evening of September 25, 1861. Several members of the black community, including Mifflin Gibbs and Nathan Pointer, were, like other Victoria businessmen, eager to support a good cause. They purchased the most expensive tickets available, tickets which admitted them to the dress circle, the best seats in the house.

As rumour spread throughout the town that blacks had purchased all the seats in the dress circle, James McCrea recognized an opportunity to have a little fun. An American auctioneer who had come to Victoria during the early days of the gold rush, McCrea became the leader of a bar-room conspiracy. The plotters, who gathered in a saloon on the evening of the performance, were determined to demonstrate to the blacks that they had taken unwelcome liberties in presuming to occupy the theatre's best seats.

McCrea began by offering fifty dollars to every performer who chose not to appear. When this tactic failed to bring about the concert's cancellation, he arranged for a bag of onions to be left at the theatre entrance, the idea being that onions hurled into the dress circle would counteract the "Ethiopian odours." If that failed to disrupt the concert or to convince the blacks to move to more humble seating, McCrea and his cohorts had another plan up their sleeves.

Mifflin Gibbs and his pregnant wife together with Nathan Pointer and his daughter took their seats in the dress circle that evening. They must have been aware that something was brewing but they were determined to ignore it. They ignored the flying onions and they ignored the loud hisses from McCrea and his friends which greeted the appearance of each performer. But by the time a bag of flour lobbed in their direction exploded on Pointer's head covering them all with flour, their blood was up.

As Pointer's daughter cried, "Oh my father, my father!" Gibbs leapt to his feet. Who did it? he demanded and then knocked to the ground the man fingered by Pointer. Pointer took a punch at another likely candidate, missed and flattened a naval officer. Before anyone was seriously hurt the police arrived to break up the melee. And to charge Gibbs and Pointer with assault.

In the days that followed the riot, the incident was debated in the pages of the *Colonist*. Emil Sutro, one of the performers who had been convinced by McCrea's munificence to cancel his appearance, explained his decision.

"I do not believe in any amalgamation of white and coloured people, nor that the latter should socially intermix with the former," he wrote.[36]

THEATRE ROYAL, *Government Street. Scene of the race riot of 1861, the Theatre Royal, the large building in the center of the picture, stood near the corner of Bastion Street.*

Emil Sutro was an easy target. A German-born Jew he had come to Victoria to operate a cigar shop for his brother Adolph, a successful San Francisco tobacconist. "It would be well if Mr. Sutro would remember that he himself belongs to a much persecuted race . . . Remembering this, his sympathies should have been with, not against, the coloured people," a correspondant who used the pen name "An Offended Englishwoman," wrote.

"Not one *respectable* person took part in the assault," she continued, adding that the attack on Gibbs and Pointer was "offensive to Englishmen" and "unwarrantable in an English Colony where all classes are truly free."

Not all of her compatriots shared her outrage. Englishman Robert Shaw, an off-duty sailor, had been easily recruited by McCrea and may have been the man who threw the flour at Gibbs and Pointer. British-born clergyman, Matthew Macfie, exhibited an interest in race so consuming as to suggest obsession. He was fascinated by the "mixed population" he discovered in Victoria.

"Among the many remarkable matrimonial alliances to be met with, I have known Europeans married to pure squaws, Indian half-breeds and Mulatto females respectively," he reported.[38] "One case has come under my observation of a negro married to a white woman, and another of a man descended from a Hindoo mother married to a wife of Indian extraction."

His mind whirling as he contemplated the "twenty-three *crosses*, in different degrees resulting from the blending of the Caucasian, the aboriginal Indian and the negro," Macfie turned his attention to James and Amelia Douglas. "A gentleman of large property, reported to be of Mulatto origin, is married to a half-breed Indian," he gasped.

Blacks were well aware that not all Englishmen were without prejudice. And even those who appeared to be more fair-minded might simply be more subtle.

"In some places of public accommodation, such as barbershops, barrooms, restaurants and hotels, colored persons are denied the usual privileges," a black visitor reported in 1864. "But such places are invariably run by Americans or foreigners. In many of the finest establishments, where the proprietors are Englishmen, there is no distinction; they are free from prejudices which Americans have introduced. There are, however, many Englishmen who are as full of prejudice as the lowest secesh (secessionist) American among them. They all, moreover, receive you with an aristocratic, patronizing air."[39]

MIFFLIN GIBBS. *Free-born in Philadelphia, Mifflin Gibbs was one of Victoria's most outspoken and influential blacks. He left the Colony in 1870. Three years later he became the first black man in the U.S. to be elected municipal judge.*

But even if they were patronized and excluded from some social events, most blacks considered themselves better off in Victoria than they had been in San Francisco. The theatre riot would not be the last racial incident to occur in the city, but it did mark the peak of racial tensions. As naturalized British subjects they had a right to vote. Since they were not British-born, they were ineligible for election to the colonial assembly, but they had the right to run for positions on Victoria's city council. In Victoria's first civic election Mifflin Gibbs was one of fourteen candidates who sought election to the six member council. He placed seventh, losing by only four votes. Later he would try again, win a seat and be appointed to serve as chairman of the important finance committee.

Mifflin Gibbs and many other blacks would join the flood of Americans deserting the colony in the last years of the 1860's. And with the departure of Americans, both black and white, Victoria's Englishness would become the city's most noticeable characteristic.

III. Capital City

1.
"general despondency and depression"

The end of the American Civil War coincided with the collapse of the Cariboo mines. The two events combined to suggest to many of Victoria's American residents that it was time to go home. The first to leave were the "Southern renegades" who had chosen to sit out the war in Victoria. They were joined by some American blacks who had never felt comfortable in a British colony and who could now travel in any of the forty-eight states as free men. Others delayed their decision to leave. They shared with Allen Francis the opinion that, had it not been for the "adventurous spirit and enterprise of Americans," the colony would have remained in "nominal obscurity." Growing increasingly impatient with the "old fogies" who seemed determined to shackle free-wheeling enterprise, these Americans hung on, reluctant to turn their backs on their Victoria investments. But finally a series of events convinced them that the British officials who controlled the future of the colony had determined to follow a path that would lead to economic ruin.

The gold discoveries that had precipitated Victoria's boom had taken place on the mainland, in British Columbia rather than within the bounds of the island colony. In 1858 when British Columbia had begun to fill with Americans, James Douglas had taken it upon himself to declare that the area was within his jurisdiction and that the same rules and regulations that applied on Vancouver Island prevailed in British Columbia. The British government supported his actions; the Colony of British Columbia was formed and James Douglas was sworn in as governor on November 19, 1858.

The two colonies existed, side-by-side but as separate entities, their only connection being James Douglas who, because of circumstances rather than by design, served as governor of both. When Douglas retired in 1864, he was replaced by two men: Arthur Kennedy became governor of Vancouver Island and Frederick Seymour assumed responsibility for British Columbia.

In April 1864 when Seymour arrived at New Westminster, the mainland capital on the banks of the lower Fraser, he carried special instructions from London. Because both colonies were slipping dangerously into debt, Seymour was to bring about the union of Vancouver Island and British Columbia as soon as possible.

By 1859 the gold rush on the lower Fraser had peaked. The pendulum had begun its predictable swing from high-flying optimism to grinding depression, when, in 1861, the richest find of all was discovered at Antler Creek. But Antler Creek was in the Cariboo, deep in the interior. Boats could travel on the Fraser only as far as Yale, the steamer landing a hundred miles from the Fraser's mouth. Above Yale the river, churning through narrow, steep-sided canyons, was impassable. To provide access to the Cariboo mines, Douglas ordered the construction of the Cariboo Wagon Road. Originally the work of a detachment of Royal Engineers, the road was an engineering masterpiece, its route so carefully selected that it continues to be followed by modern highways. Blasted out of canyon walls, crossing bridges that seemed suspended from the sky, and eventually stretching more than three hundred miles to the town of Barkerville, it was also expensive. The expense had seemed justified when it was crowded with thousands of gold-seekers and when express wagons, crammed with all manner of goods shipped through Victoria, carried supplies and the mails to growing towns along its route.

But by 1864 the tide had begun to turn. The best claims had been staked and much of the most easily found gold had been sluiced into pans, poured into bags and had departed the colony. Victoria felt the effect almost immediately, as men, discouraged and poorer than when they had set out, went home rather than returning to Victoria with the coming of winter.

There had been "a great falling off of business," Francis reported in December of 1864. The population had fallen by about 700; real estate values were plummeting; building had been suspended.[1]

If anything New Westminster's straits were even more dire. "I had not seen . . . so melancholy a picture of disappointed hopes as New Westminster presented on my arrival," Seymour recalled.[2]

'SPRINGFIELD'. *Built on Michigan Street in James Bay in the early 1860s, 'Springfield' was the home of banker Alexander Macdonald. Macdonald was in the Cariboo when his Yates Street bank was robbed in September, 1864. When unhappy investors began to suspect that he had arranged the robbery to cover his bank's insolvency, Macdonald slipped away to San Francisco, leaving his house, most of his possessions and all of his creditors behind.*

The following year the situation had become even worse. Victoria was accustomed to a revival of business during the fall and winter months but the fall of 1865 had brought nothing but "general despondency and depression." Merchants were being forced into bankruptcy and to escape creditors residents were leaving the colony clandestinely. Only four buildings had been erected during the year and rents had fallen by half. Formerly three steamships a month had arrived from San Francisco but by 1865 they had been withdrawn and only sailing vessels served the Victoria route. The population which the year earlier had been as high as 8000 had now fallen to about 3500.

"No city on the Pacific Coast occupies a more deplorable condition commercially than Victoria," Francis concluded.

Both colonies were staggering under the unbearable load of debt. With revenues falling the colonies could no longer afford the luxury of two governors, two legislatures, two attorneys-general, and the twinning of a host of other colonial officials.

On August 6, 1866 Queen Victoria put her signature to *An Act for the Union of the Colony of Vancouver Island with the Colony of British Columbia*. When they read the act, many Victorians who had supported the union, were sent reeling with dismay. Vancouver Island was not being united with British Columbia. It was being annexed. The governor of the enlarged colony would be Frederick Seymour, British Columbia's governor. Where the statutes of the two colonies differed, those passed by Vancouver Island would remain in force only until they were supplanted by new legislation. Throughout the gold rush years, Victoria had been a free port. With the Act of Union, the city lost that status and Victorians feared that their city might soon lose its commercial pre-eminence. Most worrying was the silence of the Act on the subject of the capital of the new colony. The decision would be left to Frederick Seymour.

The years 1866 - 1868, during which the location of the capital was debated, were the most crucial in the city's history. More than the participants could have guessed, Victoria's role as the capital city would prove to be not simply important but absolutely essential to the city's economic survival. For two years Victoria's fate hung in the balance, its future depending on the final decision of a governor who was known to favour New Westminster and who, many were coming to suspect, was also alcoholic.

2.
"cocktails all day"

At first Frederick Seymour had been seen simply as an hospitable man who liked to entertain but gradually it had become apparent that strong spirits rather than good spirits were the source of his obvious bonhomie. A guest at Seymour's table noted that his host was intoxicated *before* sitting down to dinner. On another occasion when he was entertaining high-ranking naval officers, Seymour had been taken ill at the dinner table and had "twice to go out to retch." By 1867 it had become obvious that the governor was desperately ill and it was equally obvious to those who knew him well that this illness could be attributed to "the effect of his constant application all day to stimulants." The Colonial Secretary considered it prudent to warn the governor's medical advisor, "In a short time you will have to give Mr. Seymour a medical certificate that he may be invalided if these cocktails all day go on as now."³

Proof of Seymour's addiction would come in June of 1869. The governor was aboard the HMS *Sparrowhawk* returning to Esquimalt after having investigated an outbreak of inter-tribal warfare among north coast Indians. On June 6, the ship's doctor found him "suffering from great gastric irritation, nervous tremors, sleeplessness and other symptoms of alcoholism."⁴ The doctor took steps to wean the governor from strong drink. His manservant was instructed to restrict Seymour's intake to a tablespoon of brandy every hour. During the night of June 9, he dozed off and was awakened by a "strange gurgling sound" coming from the governor's bed. He sprang to his feet as Seymour swallowed the dregs of a bottle of brandy and fell insensible on his bed. By ten o'clock in the morning he was dead. (*site 59*)

GOVERNOR FREDERICK SEYMOUR. *Seymour felt that he was not "extremely unpopular" with Victorians. "If he only knew the general opinion," Dr. Helmcken wrote, "he would blush."*

From 1866 to 1868, Seymour had hesitated to name the capital. He had hoped that the members of the legislature would vote in favour of New Westminster allowing him to appear to be succumbing to the wishes of the people rather than imposing his will. But his delay allowed Dr. Helmcken, former governor Douglas, and other Victorians to rally support for the city in London and in British Columbia. When the question rose in the legislature on April 2, 1868, the lobbyists were fairly confident that they commanded enough votes to secure Victoria's selection, but just to be sure they adopted a tactic as expedient as it was unparliamentary.

William Hales Franklyn, the member for Nanaimo, was known to favour New Westminster. Genial and near-sighted, Franklyn was also known to take an occasional drop of whiskey. Before the debate began, the Victoria faction had invited Franklyn to fight the morning chill with hot water and whiskey and by the time he rose to deliver his speech in support of New Westminster he was "a little shaky." After stumbling through the first page of his speech several times, apparently without noticing that he was repeating himself but aware that his remarks were not producing the response he had expected, he removed his spectacles and laid them on the table. While Franklyn gazed myopically around the assembly hoping for some sign of support, a Victoria supporter reached over and popped the lenses out of his glasses. As Franklyn stared at his papers puzzled that he could no longer make out his own writing, Helmcken moved to adjourn and during the recess the Victoria faction shepherded Franklyn to the bar and plied him with more whiskey. When the vote was taken that afternoon, Franklyn was unable to cast a vote either for or against New Westminster.

The Victoria supporters carried the day and Seymour agreed that Victoria would be named the capital of the colony on the Queen's birthday. He now had to contemplate the unpleasant prospect of leaving New Westminster and moving to Government House in Victoria, to Cary Castle a building he considered barely habitable.

During Douglas' term in office, government house had been his own residence on the banks of James Bay. When Arthur Kennedy arrived to take Douglas' place in 1864, he discovered that there was no official residence and that the legislature was reluctant to vote the funds to provide him with one. While the legislature debated the question of his residence, Kennedy rented 'Fairfield', the "prettily situated" home of Joseph Trutch who was planning to spend some months in England. (*site 50*) By April, 1865 the legislature had voted $50,000 for the governor's residence but no site had been selected and Kennedy was unwilling to while away another year in rented accommodations waiting for the construction of a new building. He let it be known that he had purchased "Castle Cary" and that he felt that after extensive alterations it would serve quite well as Government House.

CARY CASTLE. *Built in the early 1860's, Cary Castle, enlarged and remodelled several times, served as Government House until it was destroyed by fire in 1899.*

It must have been the splendid view that attracted Kennedy to Cary Castle, that and the twenty-five acres on which it sat, for the building itself was decidedly odd — a characteristic it shared with its builder, George Hunter Cary, the erratic and eccentric Attorney-General of Vancouver Island. There were those who said that in Cary genius and madness were closely allied and few doubted that madness had inspired him to build a castle, especially a castle sited on a bleak, gale-swept rocky hill, "exposed to every wind that blows."

When his shares in the Cariboo's "Never Sweat Mine" did not produce the expected returns, Cary had been forced to compromise his dream. The castle purchased by Kennedy in 1865 was no medieval fantasy. Instead it was "a queer architectural intrusion on the wild landscape," its chief feature a tower topped with battlement-like crenellations.

Kennedy paid $19,000 for the castle and after an equal amount spent on alterations it seems to have satisfied him very well during the year that was left of his tenure as governor. But Frederick Seymour was less easily pleased. He found the house "damp" and its situation "bleak." The "unsightly pile" was, Seymour opined, "unsuitable for the residence of persons in a delicate state of health."[5] No one, however, cited Cary Castle as the cause when Seymour died five months after taking up residence.

Once their city had been named the capital and the reluctant governor had moved into Cary Castle, most British residents of Victoria were content. Nothing now seemed likely to threaten Victoria's role as British Columbia's largest, most important city. Victoria's future had been secured.

Many American residents did not share their optimism. They remained convinced Victoria's economic salvation lay with the United States.

3.
"annexation"

"I am satisfied by personal observation, as well as public remarks and newspaper comments that the people of Vancouver Island . . . are almost unanimous in the desire for annexation to the United States," Allen Francis had reported in September of 1866. The only residents opposed to the notion were government officials and their families.

Carefully clipping newspaper accounts of public meetings held to discuss annexation which he then forwarded to the Secretary of State as part of his private, unofficial correspondence, and obviously excited at the prospect of being instrumental in adding to American possessions, Francis had misread the city's mood. Much of the annexation talk had erupted only after Victorians had learned of the terms of the *Act of Union* and represented a negotiating ploy in the battle for the capital rather than an earnest desire to join the American union.

In 1869 American residents made one last attempt to bring about annexation. British Columbians were now actively negotiating the union of the colony with the Confederation of Canadian provinces in the east. It seemed nothing less than folly to seek union with a distant dominion when British Columbia was sandwiched between Washington Territory and Alaska, purchased from the Russians two years earlier.

In November, 1869 a petition signed by "forty prominent business men" was forwarded to President Ulysses S. Grant. "The petition is very strongly worded, setting forth with much force and cogency of reasoning, the isolated and helpless condition of the colony, and the imperative necessity for forming a political alliance with its powerful and more prosperous neighbour," a San Francisco newspaper breathlessly reported.[6]

The petition had less than forty signatures, "principally those of foreigners," the *Colonist* sniffed.

While President Grant announced that he had received the petition with "great interest," no direct action was taken by the American administration. In 1871, the colony of British Columbia became the fifth province of the Dominion of Canada and Victoria became the provincial capital. Any lingering hopes that Victoria and Vancouver Island might one day come under American jurisdiction were dashed and the town's residents whose loyalties belonged south of the forty-ninth or who could no longer cope with the listless British approach to business, became part of the second wave of Americans to depart the city after the gold rush.

JAMES McCREA. *A realtor and auctioneer, McCrea left Victoria in 1869. Twelve years later he met an untimely, but not altogether inappropriate, end.*

James McCrea, the man who had incited the race riot in 1861, did not sign the annexation petition. He had left Victoria in March, six months before the petition was circulated. In 1881 it was reported that he had been "foully murdered" in New Mexico. Appropriately enough McCrea met his end when he remonstrated with a cowboy who was creating a disturbance in a public place. Irritated by McCrea's chiding, the man drew his gun.

"Will she pop?" McCrea asked.

"You bet she'll pop; just listen," the man cried and blew McCrea's brains out.[7]

Emil Sutro, who had been persuaded by McCrea to refuse to perform before a black audience, had signed the annexation petition. In 1875 he left the city for San Francisco and Virginia City, Nevada where his brother Adolph was making a fortune developing the silver mines of the Comstock Lode.

The Nevada silver mines would also make a millionaire out of William Sharon. In 1858 Sharon had come to Victoria from San Francisco and had opened a little shop on Yates Street where he sold sashes and blinds, dressed lumber and hardware. Discouraged by the downturn in business, he return-

75

ed to California, invested in mining stocks and by 1874 was worth an estimated $12,000,000 and lived in a San Francisco house described as being "the most magnificent private establishment on the continent."[8]

Mifflin Gibbs survived the theatre "flouring" to serve several terms as a member of Victoria's city council. Gibbs had been appalled by Governor Seymour, "the personification of official imbecility," and by the government which, he said, was "sitting like a nightmare on the energies of the people." He remained in the city until 1870 when he joined the deserting tide. A supporter of Confederation, he had been optimistic that business would improve after British Columbia became a province but he left nonetheless. "Love of home and country asserted itself," Gibbs wrote, speaking of himself but perhaps also for many other departing Americans.[9]

4.
"a weather-beaten antique appearance"

In 1871, the year British Columbia entered Confederation and Victoria became the provincial capital, the population of the city had shrunk to 3,270. The business district, over-built during the gold rush, remained confined to a few square blocks. Few repairs or improvements had been made and downtown buildings had assumed a "weather-beaten antique appearance." But the town's progress had not halted altogether.

In 1871 hotel-keeper Sosthenes Driard purchased the St. George Hotel, added a mansard roof and 34 rooms, and warmed to the *Colonist's* description of his achievement. "Outside of San Francisco the Driard Hotel has no rival in point of beauty, of location or accommodation on the Pacific Coast."[10] (*site 20*)

The federal government added two imposing structures to the cityscape; an Italianate Post Office built in 1873 on the Government Street site once occupied by Governor Blanshard's house and a Custom House completed in 1875. (*site 15*)

Close-by the business district, along Fort, Yates and Johnson Streets, one- and two-story wooden houses, some unabashedly unadorned, others decorated with bargeboard and topped with finials, stood in neatly fenced gardens, most no larger than two or three city lots. "Their homes are plain, comfortable and inexpensive," a visitor noted.[11] A few houses had been built east of Cook Street — along Belcher Street, which rose to the heights topped by Cary Castle, and along Fort Street, which changed its name to Cadboro Bay Road just east of Cook and wandered through the countryside out to John Tod's Oak Bay farm and on to Cadboro Bay.

To the north and east of town, property was in the hands of men who counted their holdings in the hundreds of acres. Fernwood, Gonzales, Cloverdale, Hillside and other estates would become closely built communities thirty or forty years later, but in 1871 they remained largely unimproved and occupied by only a few families.

JACOB HUNTER TODD HOUSE, *Johnson Street near Vancouver. Built in the 1870's with the profits he made from his
Barkerville general store, Todd's house was demolished in 1959
and replaced by a funeral parlour.*

'DUVALS', *1462 Rockland Avenue. Built early in the 1860's,
'Duvals' adopted the Country Gothic style popular in the United
States.*

'WENTWORTH VILLA', *1156 Fort Street. Built in 1862 for Martha Cheney and her husband Henry Ella, 'Wentworth Villa', with fourteen rooms and nine fireplaces, was the largest and most luxurious
private residence in the Colony. One of Victoria's oldest houses, it
survives today as an antique shop.*

'TREGEW'. *Built in 1860 or 1861, 'Tregew' stood at 436 Michigan until 1967 when it was demolished to make way for an apartment building.*

By 1871 the only area that could be considered a residential neighbourhood was the James Bay district. The Hudson's Bay Company had released its hold on Beckley Farm and opened its acres for purchase. After the James Bay bridge connected Beckley Farm with the business district, the land had become an obvious choice for home-builders who wanted to be close to town. Some built on the city-sized lots that ringed the Inner Harbour. The remainder of James Bay had been divided into large properties of two, four and as many as ten and twenty acres. On these country-sized properties houses were built tucked in forest clearings. The design of these houses and the materials with which they were built more than hinted at their owners' backgrounds and traditions.

Some British residents, continuing to be distrustful of the lasting qualities of wood, built homes of brick or stone. Thomas Trounce, a Cornish-born architect, chose stone for 'Tregew', its two-foot-thick walls a vast improve-

RICHARD CARR HOUSE, *207 Government Street. The birth place of Emily Carr, the house is one of only a few early James Bay homes to have escaped demolition.*

78

ment over the Douglas Street tent he and his wife had lived in when they first arrived in 1858. Alexander Macdonald, a Scot, built his house of stout red brick. Others, who had spent some time in San Francisco and had become familiar with the charm of the redwood villas of the East Bay, were more than content to build California-style houses. English-born Richard Carr, who built his house on four acres near Beacon Hill Park, directed architect John Wright to prepare plans for an Italian-villa residence which would have settled quite comfortably into Alameda or Berkeley. Carr saw no contradiction in surrounding his American-style house with an English garden. (*site 34*)

"The English character of the place is particularly noticeable," an American visitor recorded in 1875.[12] But he was talking about the mood, rather than the appearance, of the town. Compared to American towns on the Pacific Coast with their "restless, energetic, driving people who seem hardly to know what rest and relaxation mean, Victoria seems almost lifeless in business."

"The people of the town seem to live for the sake of enjoying their journey through this world instead of rushing through existence like a rocket," he continued, becoming one of the first visitors to recognize and be charmed by the city's aura of contented serenity.

But appearances could be deceiving, for, during the seventies some Victorians, who had been quietly amassing fortunes, would begin to build the imposing residences — the castles, the gothic fantasies, the rambling country villas and the eclectic Queen Annes, which suggested studied elegance or exubrant free-spending eccentricity and which would add some authenticity to Victoria's claim that it rivalled San Francisco.

The men, who survived the economic depression that settled over Victoria for almost twenty years and who used their wealth to create a charmed society and an enticingly beautiful city, fell into three categories. They were retired HBC officers. They were members of the professional class who had enjoyed the benefits of colonial appointments. And increasingly they were self-made men.

'ARMADALE'. *Built in James Bay in 1877 for William Macdonald, 'Armadale' was surrounded by a twenty-eight acre estate. After the house was demolished in 1944, part of its grounds were retained as Macdonald Park.*

IV. Society

1.
"improved Scots"

Old fur traders, men like Douglas, Tolmie, and Finlayson, were the largest land-holders in the community. James Douglas had been among the first to purchase land when the Fur Trade Reserve in the vicinity of the fort was opened for sale to colonists in 1852. His Fairfield Farm Estate stretched from Beacon Hill Park to Ross Bay Cemetery and from the waterfront as far north as Fort Street. Rather than sell his land in small parcels as the town began to grow and spread in his direction, Douglas chose to dole out his property to a variety of long-term leaseholders. Cary Castle was built on property leased from Douglas and later from his heirs, the lease-hold agreement remaining in effect until it was extinguished by mutual agreement in 1922 long after the property had become Government House.[1]

In 1864 when he retired as governor of the two colonies, Douglas was knighted by Queen Victoria. The Knight Commander of Bath and particularly Lady Douglas did not become leaders of society. Sensitive to old insults, Amelia, "a dear old soul," chose to spend her days fussing over her house, her garden and her chickens.

"Mama is in excellent health, though she will not think so," Douglas wrote to his daughter Martha, attending school in England. "Up every morning at 6, she bustles till breakfast time. The chickens now fill her mind with anxious care, and we all look grave and appear to sympathize if mishaps occur. To laugh would be a serious offense."[2]

Slipping outside to smoke his pipe because Amelia forbade the activity inside the house and getting exercise by skipping rope on his verandah, Douglas devoted most of his time to the management of his estate. "I enjoy with keenest relish the quiet pleasures of my own fireside," Douglas wrote, in terms that suggested contented retirement. But John Tod, who had known Douglas since the time he had been William Connolly's clerk, cast Douglas' retreat from political and social affairs in a different light.

"Friend Douglas has of late become very unsteady of step, shaky of head

JAMES DOUGLAS. *Douglas had little cause to worry about his finances. In 1869 his income from property and investments was $27,500 while living expenses were less than $5000.*

and dim of eye," he wrote in 1870.[3] The older Douglas became, Tod said, the more concerned he became with his financial position. "Notwithstanding his ample means, he is as eager and grasping after money as ever and . . . at times is seized with gloomy apprehensions of dying a beggar at last."

"To all those who have known him for years," Tod continued, "he has appeared cold, crafty and selfish, and justly merits the rewards he now reaps of isolation and desertion of all who have known him from the early times."

John Work of Hillside Farm died in 1861, too early to witness the social success of his daughters and too early to grieve over the failure of his sons. Of the eleven children John's wife Josette bore him, only three were sons. Henry, the youngest, died accidentally in 1856 when he was twelve. Neither of the other two, John born in 1839 and David, ten years his junior, were regarded as having amounted to much.

"It is rather remarkable," John Tod mused, "that so numerous a family of daughters should have all turned out so well, their exemplary good conduct having gained the universal esteem and respect of their neighbours, and the only two sons who survived their father should have displayed characteristics quite the reverse."[4]

John's problem was alcohol; David's problem was undiagnosed, but to Tod at least its effects were apparent. "The family," Tod wrote, "seem overwhelmed with grief at the reckless profligacy of the elder son . . . the other son, although sufficiently temperate, as regards Drink, is yet in my opinion, a much more despicable character than his brother."[5]

David died in his thirty-first year when he was seized by a fit and fell dead upon the deck of a steamer travelling up the Columbia River. John, who managed Hillside Farm for his mother, died at forty-six of "dropsy."

JOSETTE WORK WITH SUZETTE AND DAVID. *Like the other daughters of John and Josette Work, Suzette did rather well, marrying Edward Gawler Prior who became one of the two men who have served as both Premier and Lieutenant-Governor of British Columbia. Like his brother John, David was a disappointment.*

One of Work's daughters, whom Tod had praised as having turned out so well, married Dr. William Fraser Tolmie. Born in Inverness in 1812 and trained as a doctor at Glasgow University, he joined the Company in 1832. Tolmie spent most of his years with the Company stationed at Fort Nisqually in Washington Territory. He was the first white man to attempt to climb Mount Rainier and a peak on the mountain was later named Tolmie Peak in his honour.

After years of agonizing over the advisability of taking a half-breed wife, Tolmie married Jane Work in 1850. Having decided to remain in the west rather than return to Scotland after he retired from the Company, Tolmie purchased "country land" adjacent to his father-in-law's holdings. By 1858 he had begun to work his eleven hundred-acre farm and the following year, when the Company moved him to Fort Victoria, he began construction of his house.

Designed by architect John Wright, 'Cloverdale' was built in three stages, each with a different building material and all blended into a whole by a light covering of roughcast stucco. The main part of the house, containing some two thousand square feet, was built of stone quarried on the site. The sills of the windows which were set into the two-foot thick walls were made of sandstone collected on Salt Spring Island. Doors and decorative mouldings were California redwood imported from San Francisco. An attached kitchen, which also contained the Tolmies' breakfast room, was built of hand-hewn logs, salvaged by Tolmie when the HBC buildings within the fort were being dismantled. A third wing, seventy-five feet long, was built of inch-thick redwood boards and served as the farm's storage room.

'CLOVERDALE'. *Tolmie's house which stood on Lovat Avenue was demolished in 1963. "We want to get it down before anyone knows about it," the developer said. "The historical people have been driving me crazy."*

Tolmie took an active interest in politics. "When I was a boy," his son, Simon Fraser Tolmie, recalled, "I used to drive my father to town on Saturdays and I sat for hours outside newspaper offices and other places while he was talking politics."[6]

Recognized as an ethnologist and historian and as being public-spirited and progressive, Tolmie was a staunch supporter of the public school system and served for many years on the board of education. In his own home, he demonstrated the importance he placed on a good education.

"One of his favorite sayings was that an hour in the morning was worth two at night," his son remembered. "We usually retired at 9 p.m. We arose at 5 in the morning and foregathered in the library at 5:20 a.m., and there we would go over my lessons for the day." His lessons over at seven, he would set off for school. Travelling three-quarters of a mile before he had left his own property, he spent almost three hours a day walking to and from school. The discipline of those early days paid off. Simon Fraser Tolmie became a veterinarian and later entered politics. In 1928 he became British Columbia's first native-born premier.

In 1849 Sarah, another of John Work's daughters married Roderick

·Finlayson, the young HBC officer who had assumed command of Fort Victoria after Charles Ross' death. After Douglas arrived to direct the affairs of the fort, Finlayson was appointed chief accountant and for a time he and Sarah lived in rooms attached to his office in Fort Victoria where Sarah was kept busy protecting her chickens from the Indian dogs which swam across the inlet with supper in mind. After 1852 when the HBC released land within the Fur Trade Reserve for sale, Finlayson acquired a large holding south of John Work's land and over the years he became one of the largest property owners in the city.

After he left the Company's service in 1872, Finlayson lived off his land, the income he collected from leases allowing him to be considered one of Victoria's "wealthiest and most prominent citizens." He was not, however, considered one of the city's brightest residents. "He thought he could successfully conclude any argument with the words, 'But I have seen it in print'," an acquaintance recalled.[7]

RODERICK FINLAYSON HOUSE. *Finlayson's house, which was later doubled in size, stood on Douglas Street south of Bay Street.*

Whatever his intellectual shortcomings, Finlayson was elected mayor of the city in 1878 and it was during his administration that the architect's plans that had been gathering dust for three years were finally acted upon and Victoria's City Hall was built. (*site 29*)

Fur-trade families, land-rich and enjoying some status for having been the first on the scene, didn't quite measure up to the standards of the more recently arrived Englishmen. Because his wife had Indian blood, Dr. Helmcken was considered "not quite a gentleman." Charles Bayley, marginally literate and appointed a colonial schoolmaster, could peer down his nose at "the rude customs and manners of the employes [sic] of the Company."

"It was not," Bayley claimed, "till the introduction of white men from the old country that they became civilized."[8]

A generation and more would pass before the sly joke lost its sting. The traders' children with their mixture of Scottish and Indian blood were, Englishmen quipped, "improved Scots."

2.
"a horde of inexperienced men"

Soon after the Colony of Vancouver Island was formed in 1849, the Colonial Office in London began to recruit young men — lawyers, engineers, surveyors, policemen — who would become the colony's first civil servants and colonial administrators. The gold rush and the formation of the Colony of British Columbia in 1858 brought a second wave of London-recruited officials to the west coast. To Americans, who felt responsible for discovering the gold and developing the mines, they were "a horde of inexperienced men" who enacted and enforced "onerous" laws.[9] But however onerous the laws seemed and however inexperienced the men may have been, they brought to the British Columbia gold rush a sense of order and a lack of the lawlessness that had characterized the California rush. And when the excitement was over, many of them were on their way to amassing considerable fortunes.

Joseph Despard Pemberton was thirty years old when he arrived at Fort Victoria in 1851. Born in Dublin, he was the grandson of a mayor of the Irish city. He studied civil engineering at Trinity College, Dublin and was a professor of engineering and mathematics at an English agricultural college when he was recruited by the HBC to serve as Colonial Surveyor replacing the hapless Captain Grant.

He reached Fort Victoria in June and, after having re-done the surveys attempted by Grant, he was assigned the task of laying out and surveying the townsite around the fort. By January, 1852 the townsite plans were ready to be forwarded to London and Pemberton spent the next three years exploring, surveying and mapping Saanich, Cowichan, the Nanaimo district and other up-island locales. When he made the decision to make the Island his permanent home he probably knew it better than any man.

In 1855 he returned to England where he collected his sister Susan and his "youngest and most favorite" uncle. Born in Dublin in 1808, Augustus Frederick Pemberton was only thirteen years older than Joe. He regarded him as a brother rather than a nephew and was easily persuaded to give up his legal career and sign an agreement whereby he would manage a farm to be financed by Joe in return for half the profits.[10]

James Douglas had recommended that the thousand acre estate which made up the Governor's Reserve be opened for sale. The Pembertons became the first to profit from that decision, when in 1856 they purchased Gonzalo the two hundred acre dairy farm that the HBC had operated within the reserve.[11] Gonzalo was only the first of a series of properties acquired by Joe Pemberton. Eventually he would own more than half of the land in the Oak Bay district.

"It was Sir James Douglas who made us rich by insisting upon our taking up land," a friend of the Pembertons later recalled and one young Company employee would discover to his dismay that it was advice Joe Pemberton intended to follow.[12]

JOSEPH D. PEMBERTON   AUGUSTUS F. PEMBERTON

William Macdonald, a native of Inverness, had arrived at Fort Victoria in 1851. A few years before he left the Company's service in 1858, he was urged by Douglas to buy land near Oak Bay. Hesitating, wanting more advice before he made a decision, he called on Joe Pemberton at the land office. The Governor had recommended Oak Bay to him, Macdonald said. What did the surveyor think? Pemberton was non-committal and so Macdonald hied himself out to Oak Bay, walked over the land and decided that the magnificent views more than compensated for the rocky outcrops that divided the arable acres.

"I went to the land office and informed Mr. Pemberton of my decision," Macdonald recalled. "Mr. Pemberton, rubbing his nose in his usual manner, replied 'I have taken it myself'."

"Passionately fond of horses" and a bold rider, Joe Pemberton was thrown from his horse while galloping along the Esquimalt Road. The injuries he suffered, which would affect him for the rest of his life, prompted him to resign from the colonial service in 1864. He went to England for a recuperative holiday, collected a bride and returned to Victoria to devote himself to the improvement of his twelve hundred acre land holdings.

In 1885 he spent $10,000 to build 'Gonzales', a mansion of twenty rooms, including a billiard room, a library, a writing room, a conservatory and an entrance hall of six hundred square feet. Here Pemberton led "the quiet life of a country gentleman," devoting himself to breeding Clydesdale horses and shorthorn cattle and emerging from peaceful self-imposed obscurity to perform public benefactions, one of which included designing, surveying, building and gifting the government with Oak Bay Avenue which ran for its entire length through Pemberton's property.

It was on Oak Bay Avenue, in 1893 when he was seventy-two that Joe Pemberton met his death. He and his wife Teresa were riding home together after a Hunt Club paper chase. Joe was lagging behind and Teresa had left the avenue and was moving along Cadboro Bay Road when she looked back, impatient for Joe to catch up. His body was lying on the ground. He had been catapulted from his horse by a violent heart attack.

'GONZALES'. *Built in 1885 near the corner of Rockland Avenue and St. Charles Street, 'Gonzales' was demolished in 1952 after it had served for many years as Norfolk House School.*

Although he had come to Vancouver Island fully intending to devote himself to farming, Augustus Pemberton, like his nephew Joe, benefited from a colonial appointment. For two years, Augustus worked at Gonzalo, clearing more land and adding to the small log cabin that had come with the property. In 1858 as the town filled with Fraser-bound miners, Douglas appointed Pemberton Commissoner of Police. Credited with being responsible for the preservation of law and order in the town, Pemberton also served as Magistrate of the Police Court which convened in the Police Barracks court room where he had the pleasure of jailing Attorney-General Cary for having participated in a duel, but where he usually found himself passing judgement on a series of petty criminals: thieves, drunks, street-fighters and deserting sailors.

A life-long friend of both Pembertons, Benjamin William Pearse was just nineteen years old when he arrived at Fort Victoria in 1851. Born in Devonshire in 1832, and with some training in civil engineering, he had been engaged to serve as assistant surveyor under Joseph Pemberton. Like Pemberton, Pearse soon decided to make the colony his permanent home. Some time before 1858, he purchased three hundred acres about two miles from the fort. Of an evening Pearse would walk out to his land, scramble atop a rocky hummock, and smoke a quiet pipe while he planned his house. One evening, he would later recall, he had been meditating between puffs when it suddenly occurred to him that he could build his house out of the stone on which he was sitting. 'Fernwood' was completed in 1860 and for the following forty years, Pearse lovingly improved his home adding black marble facings to some fireplaces and fine porcelain tiles to others, installing mother-of-pearl inlays to newel posts and lining the walls of some of his rooms with lavishly decorated panels of pressed tin. By 1891 the house had matured in its setting. It was, one visitor recalled, "covered with honey suckle, ivy and roses, almost embowered in beautiful flowers, surrounded by grand old oaks and firs and a small domain of park and lawn, through which wind well-kept roads and paths, rendered more attractive by the moss-grown banks and ferny dells."[13]

'FERNWOOD'. *Giving its name to the Fernwood area of Victoria, Benjamin Pearse's house stood near the corner of Fort and Fern Street.*

But 'Fernwood', during its first years at least, was not a happy house. In 1862 Pearse married Mary Laetitia Pemberton, a cousin of Joe Pemberton. She died, childless, in 1872 after having been an invalid for some years and was the first person to be buried in Ross Bay Cemetery. (*site 38*) Four years after Mary Laetitia's death, Pearse married Sarah Jane Palmer and together they produced a daughter Mary. Both Mary and her father died in 1902 and Sarah Jane lived on in 'Fernwood' alone for the next fifty-two years. One hundred years old when she died, Sarah Jane Pearse had been mistress of 'Fernwood' for seventy-eight years.

Joseph Trutch, a civil engineer like Pemberton and Pearse, came to the colony by a slightly different route. Born in Somerset in 1826, Trutch signed a contract to build an iron warehouse in San Francisco and arrived on the west coast in 1850. Other contracts took him to Oregon and Illinois, but by 1858 he decided he didn't care for the United States and returned to England with Julia Hyde, his American-born wife. In England he met Colonel Moody, the officer in charge of a party of Royal Engineers, who was about to leave England for British Columbia. The Trutchs arrived at Victoria on May 26, 1859 and two months later, as a result of Moody's recommendation, Trutch received a $10,000 contract from Governor Douglas to survey lots on the lower Fraser. In 1861 he received a $50,000 contract to build portions of the Cariboo Road and in 1863 he built the Alexandra Suspension Bridge which crossed the Fraser on a site selected by the Royal Engineers. Trutch was given a seven-year license to collect tolls on the bridge, a concession which would bring him an annual income of $20,000.

SARAH JANE PEARSE. *During a time when families remained in one place, it was not uncommon for a widow to die in the house to which she had come a bride. When Sarah Jane died in 1954 she had been mistress of 'Fernwood' for seventy-eight years.*

In 1860 Trutch wrote to his widowed mother Charlotte who was living in England with his sister Caroline. "I have acquired a most beautiful piece of land, about ten acres on the skirts of Victoria, and commanding a lovely view," he enthused. "When I hear you are coming I shall build a nice house, large enough for us all."[14] (*site 50*)

'FAIRFIELD', *601 Trutch Street. In 1861, ten years before he was appointed British Columbia's first Lieutenant-Governor, Joseph William Trutch built 'Fairfield', designed by architect John Wright in the Italian-villa style popular for residences in the countryside around San Francisco.*

The following year he built 'Fairfield' on the acres he had leased from James Douglas and the same year Charlotte and Caroline arrived. Born in 1799 Charlotte was one of the oldest women in Victoria but she took an active part in the social life enjoyed by the city's "first families". At picnics and dinner parties she sat in state, "beautifully and daintily dressed" in lavender silk and adorned with one of the many lace caps for which she was famous.

In spite of being "bright and clever and gifted with a beautiful voice" and having made a husband-hunting trip to visit a sister whose husband was stationed in India, Caroline was a spinster when she arrived in Victoria — a state that was soon rectified after she was introduced to Peter O'Reilly at a dinner party at 'Fairfield'.

"A delightful . . . tall young Irishman," O'Reilly was a veteran of the Irish Revenue Police when he arrived on Douglas' doorstep in 1859 with a letter of introduction from the Secretary of State. Chronically short of qualified men to fill important positions, Douglas had immediately appointed him a magistrate. For the next few years O'Reilly served as magistrate, assistant gold commissioner and high sheriff in the Cariboo. In 1863, the same year he married Caroline Trutch, he was characterized, in one of Douglas' confidential reports, as "a gentleman of excellent character" and "high moral worth."[15]

After several years of rented accommodation O'Reilly and Caroline purchased 'Point Ellice', a rambling, comfortable house fronting on the waters of the Gorge, built by John Work for his daughter Kate and her husband soon after their marriage in 1861. (*site 55*) On December 31, 1867 after they had been in the house fewer than three weeks, their daughter Kathleen was born. She would remain a resident of the house until her death in 1945, seventy-eight years later.

Like O'Reilly, Montague Tyrwhitt-Drake arrived in Victoria with impeccable credentials. Born into a family which proudly traced its ancestry to a brother of Sir Francis Drake, he had been educated at Charterhouse school and admitted to the bar as a solicitor in 1851. In 1859, the same year he arrived in Victoria, he was appointed revisor of the Colony's voters list and formed a legal partnership with Attorney-General Cary.

Soon after the O'Reillys settled at 'Point Ellice', Tyrwhitt-Drake and his wife Joanna joined them in the Pleasant Street neighbourhood, building a many-gabled house set in gardens which tumbled down to the waters of the Gorge.

Of all the colonial appointees, perhaps the best-known and the most influential was Matthew Baillie Begbie. Born in 1819, Begbie was educated at Cambridge. A barrister, specializing in contract law and the interpretation of wills and trusts, Begbie had never argued a criminal case when he was apppointed to serve as Judge of British Columbia in 1858.

Begbie carried justice to the mines, travelling on horseback around the Cariboo circuit, hearing cases in the open air, sitting astride his horse or perched on a stump where no courtrooms were available. Begbie's presence, his imperious air and his insistence that English law would be firmly applied, together with the knowledge that justice would come swiftly and in a no-

nonsense manner, kept to a minimum the lawlessness and vigilantism that had characterized the California mines.

Tall and vigorous and unflaggingly energetic, Begbie revelled in the outdoor life, its only drawback being a certain a lack of social variety.

"When you write, you should write *gossip*," Begbie chided a friend in a letter written from Richfield in 1865. "I can't send you any gossip from this place — the unisexual character of the population almost precludes it."[16]

Begbie's love of gossip, endless chatter about gardens and tennis, children's bellyaches and church sermons, and his unmarried status made him immensely popular with the ladies of Victoria after he moved to the city in 1870. In 1877, two years after he was knighted by the Queen, he built a large comfortable house set in extensive grounds between Fairfield Road and Collinson Street where he fussed over his roses and prepared elaborate and sought-after invitations to the tennis parties he held on his three courts.

Matthew Begbie, the O'Reillys, the Trutchs, the Pearses and the Pembertons, together with other men who held appointed office in the two colonies, formed the city's "first families." They socialized with one another; they married into each others' families; they were lionized as the "Founders of British Columbia"and not one of them seems to have died poor.

When he died in 1894, Begbie's estate amounted to $133,000. O'Reilly's personal and real estate was valued at $98,000. Trutch left an estate of $119,000, not counting the property he owned in England. Probate files do not contain a statement of Joe Pemberton's net worth, but other evidence suggests that he may have been the most prosperous of them all. It is difficult to assess the comparative worth of nineteenth century dollars, but some notion of the wealth of the first families might be found by multiplying by a factor of ten.

3.
"an incurable idiot"

Not all colonial appointees did as well for the colonies, or as well for themselves. Captain Peter Brunton Whannell, "a dark military appearing man with black whiskers and a mustache and a young Australian wife," appeared before Governor Douglas carrying a letter which introduced him as a former officer who had served in the army in India and in an Australian cavalry regiment. Douglas, impressed by his credentials, had immediately appointed him Justice of the Peace at Yale.[17]

Bristling with military efficiency, Whannell organized the police force at Yale. He strutted about in a gaudy uniform, "his gold lace military cap tilted to one side . . . his sabre and sabretache dangling about his legs," insisting on precisely executed salutes and meeting his responsiblities with "bold, insane, reckless zeal & utter ignorance."

Eventually the announcement of his appointment made its way to a newspaper in Melbourne, Australia. And soon Douglas was informed by the

Australian authorities that Whannell had served in Melbourne, but as an enlisted man rather than as an officer and that he had departed the colony with another man's wife.

When the Governor decided to remove him from the colonial payroll, Whannell was infuriated. The charges amounted to nothing more than "a tirade of malicious falsehoods," he stormed. His character and that of his wife had been besmirched by "the angry ablutions of a distorted, malicious, vindictive and vicious mind."

But Douglas was not to be budged. Whannell left Yale and returned to Victoria where he opened a hotel, the Clifton House on Broad Street. It was not a success. Whannell, a man who often seemed to be "raging under a sense of outraged dignity," blamed its failure on lack of patronage of his own countrymen. His hotel, Whannell claimed, was the only English house of its kind in Victoria but Englishmen preferred to patronize the "French and German Establishments."

In 1861 he admitted defeat. He had, he said, been "brought up to the profession of Arms" and he found it difficult to adjust to any other life. Now he was "left without a single dollar" and unable to leave the Island. He begged friends for passage money to return to England, but their generosity extended only so far as San Francisco and it was from San Francisco, in March 1862, that Douglas received the last of a series of letters in which Whannell demanded that the Governor investigate the charges made against him. The Governor, apparently, didn't think it worth the trouble.

Charles Good was a very different man from Whannell but he too was a colonial appointee who left the country under something of a cloud. A minister's son, Good had left England soon after taking a degree at Oxford. He arrived in Victoria early in 1859 and soon afterward was appointed Chief Clerk in the Colonial Secretary's office. For a time he served as Governor Douglas' private secretary, a position which brought him into intimate contact with the governor's family. In 1861 Good ran off with Douglas' strong-headed, seventeen year old daughter Alice. The two slipped across the Sound to be married by an American Justice of the Peace at Port Townsend. On their return the following day, Douglas, faced with a *fait accompli* and uncertain about the validity of the American marriage, insisted that they go through a second ceremony and on August 31, 1861 Alice and Charles repeated their vows in Victoria.[18]

Charles Good seems to have been an adequate private secretary but a fool when it came to managing his personal financial affairs. The man was "an incurable idiot" who was "head over heels in debt," Douglas complained in 1869. In marrying Good Alice had proven herself to be a woman with a mind of her own. Now she decided to change it. Alice had taken "an inconceivable dislike to Good, so much so that she can hardly bear to see him," Douglas reported to Alice's sister. But even though he disapproved, Douglas made sure that Alice had an income of her own — just enough to keep her "in a quiet way."

In January, 1870 Alice made a bolt for freedom. Taking her three children with her, she escaped to England. She was leaving to ensure that her children received a proper education, she said, but Douglas and everyone else in Victoria knew that what she really wanted to do was get away from Good. "A most unchristian course," Douglas grumbled.

Later that year Good went to England, collected his family and brought them back to Victoria. Alice now had to cope with lectures from her father and from the Anglican bishop, both of whom insisted that she become reconciled with her husband. Alice remained adamant. "A charming girl and very lady-like," Alice concealed a world of determination under her "placid exterior."

ALICE DOUGLAS. *In 1861 when she was seventeen, James Douglas' daughter Alice eloped with his private secretary. Nine years later Douglas reported, "She hates her husband with a bitter hatred which amounts to insanity."*

Good returned to England in 1876 leaving his wife in Victoria. The following year Alice was in California where she obtained a divorce and married a man some suspected of being a bogus "Baron."

"Had she trusted her Father more, and put less faith in Good, how different, and how much more happy would her lot in life have been," Douglas sighed.

4.
"in trade"

The "first families", who would have continued to be members of the middle class had they remained in Britain, formed the nucleus of Victoria's aristocracy. They found it easy to remember that they belonged to the professional class and hard to forget that some of the families who were elbowing their way into their ranks had made their fortunes "in trade."

By 1861 Thomas Harris had built a substantial two story brick residence, acknowledged to be one of the "best" houses in Victoria. But in spite of his success, he remained an object of fun.

Lady Jane Franklin and her niece Sophia accepted an invitation to dine with the Harrises. Before their visit, George Hills, who had arrived in 1860 to assume his position as Bishop of Columbia, shared with the ladies a vignette. Soon after he arrived, the Bishop said, he had had the assets of the Colony explained to him by Harris.

"Mr. Ills — I consider this hisland to be the ghem of the hocean," the Bishop mimicked.[19]

Alerted by Hills to the class of people they would meet, they were further prepared for their visit by Lieutenant Philip Hankin of HMS *Hecate* who had been assigned by his captain to serve as Lady Franklin's aide de camp.

"When we arrive Mrs. Harris will herself open the front door and she will wear a low-necked dress with a large locket, containing a photograph of Mr. Harris around her neck," Hankin predicted.[20] "She will also wear a beautiful white cap with a bright red ribbon, and a red rose on each side of her cap."

Encouraged by Lady Franklin's delighted laughter, Hankin continued. "She will make a low bow, and say in a low whisper — wouldn't Your Ladyship like to go upstairs and wash your hands?" Hankin enjoyed himself immensely when Mrs. Harris appeared and acted just as he had said she would.

Sophia's impression of the Harrises was predictable. "They are excellent people, & likely to be among the most influential of their class, but are not blessed with over much education — more's the pity!" she confided in her journal.

Unlike Harris, a farmer's son and a self-described " 'umble tradesman," some of Victoria's entrepreneurs came from the middle class. Born in London in 1838, William Wilson had worked as an accountant for a firm of silk manufacturers.[21] After the business went bankrupt, twenty-three year old Wilson, who had read about Victoria and the gold rush in the London *Times*, decided to try his luck on the west coast. He arrived with a supply of dry goods which he quickly sold and using his profits he acquired a store. Excited by the ease with which he had established himself, he wrote encouragingly to his brother Joseph asking him to join him. The firm, re-named W. & J. Wilson, enjoyed continued success partly due to its location on Government Street opposite the post office — an excellent location for a shop since, until home delivery was begun in the 1880's, Victorians were required to call at the post office to pick up their mail. (*site 21*)

Also lured to Victoria by William Wilson's description of the town, was David Spencer.[22] Born in Wales and a committed Methodist, Spencer had apprenticed for five years with a dry goods firm when he decided to travel to Victoria in 1863. He purchased a stationery store which he ran until 1873 when he and a partner bought the Victoria House, a dry goods store near the corner of Fort and Government. Five years later the partnership disbanded and Spencer went into business on his own opening a dry goods store, which grew into a department store, on the east side of Government between Fort and View.

As his business prospered, Spencer moved his family, which increased to include thirteen children, from one house to another, each representing a step up the social scale. By the mid-seventies the Spencers had moved from their small one story cottage to a tall two-storied, gingerbread-decorated residence dramatically sited at the end of the James Bay bridge. By the turn of the century they had settled into 'Lan Dderwan', a huge cupola-topped mansion on several acres of land between Belcher and Fort Streets, a neighbourhood favoured by some of the city's first families. (*site 46*)

'LAN DDERWAN', *1040 Moss Street. Originally named 'Gyppeswyk' and surrounded by gardens, tennis courts and orchards, the house was built in 1889 for $24,000 and is now the home of the Victoria Art Gallery.*

As the possession of wealth, rather than the means by which it had been acquired, became criteria enough for social acceptance the Wilsons and the Spencers slipped easily into an enlarged aristocracy. But for Samuel Nesbitt acceptance would be more difficult to achieve.

'ERIN HALL'. *Located in extensive grounds on Carberry Gardens 'Erin Hall' burned to the ground in 1962.*

Socially Nesbitt had two strikes against him. Not only had he made his money by manufacturing crackers, biscuits and hardtack which he sold to the navy, but also his wife Jane Saunders had reached Victoria aboard the *Tynemouth*, the brideship underwritten by English philanthropists which had arrived in the harbour in 1862 carrying a cargo of single women to the wife-hungry men of Victoria.

In 1873 the biscuit-maker built 'Erin Hall'. With its ten rooms, its thirteen-foot-high ceilings, its wide black walnut staircase and its $10,000 price tag, 'Erin Hall' was an indication that Samuel Nesbitt had done rather well.[23] But not well enough to prevent some Victorians from christening the house "Cracker Castle."

SEHL HOUSE. *Jacob Sehl established a large furniture factory on Laurel Point and during the 1880's built his spectacular house nearby. It was destroyed by fire in 1894.*

After a generation passed and the children of fur-traders, professional men and self-made men had shared the common experiences of English boarding schools and continental finishing schools, early social distinctions would blur but the century would have turned before a brewer's daughter or an ironmonger's wife became chatelaines of Cary Castle. During the 1870's and 1880's, while Victoria's society had begun to homogenize, the cream remained on top.

5.
"The House of All Sorts"

Not everyone who reached Victoria during its gold-mad years became successful or did as well as the Wilsons, the Spencers, the Nesbitts or the other families who continue to be remembered because of the businesses they founded, the spectacular homes they built or the political careers they pursued. With no streets or public buildings or landmarks named after them, many ordinary men have slipped anonymously into the past. But three men have managed to cling to the pages of history, not because of their own achievements, but because of the women in their lives; Richard Carr and Duncan Cameron because of their daughters and John Howard because of his wives.

Richard Carr was British-born. He had become a successful merchant in California during the rush of '49. In 1861 he realized $30,000 from the sale of his general stores and he returned to England. He discovered that although his loyalties and values remained English, he had been too long away and he no longer felt comfortable in his homeland. He decided to move his family to Victoria where he hoped to find a society which would combine English social values with American progressiveness.

In 1863 he purchased four acres in the James Bay area and the following year he built his house.[27] Together the land and house had set him back almost $10,000 and it may be that they cost him more than he had budgeted for, because that same year he decided to sell an acre of his land adjacent to Beacon Hill Park. The purchaser soberly promised that he would not open an inn. But William Lush, calculating the amount of liquor that would be

PARK HOTEL. *Built at the corner of Government and Simcoe, the Park Hotel became a notorious watering-hole and an enduring irritation to Richard Carr. His daughter Emily recalled, "It was just a nice drive from Esquimalt . . . and hacks filled with tipsy sailors and noisy ladies drove past our house going to the Park Hotel in the daytime and at night. It hurt Father right up till he was seventy years old, when he died."*

required to quench the thirst of the cricketers and racing enthusiasts who gathered in the park, resisted temptation for only a few months before building the Park Hotel, "one of the horridest saloons in Victoria."

In 1871 when his eighth child and last daughter was born, Richard Carr, an archetypal Victorian papa who felt the whole family should quite properly revolve around him, would have dismissed as ridiculous any suggestion that she would become so famous an artist and a writer that *his* James Bay house would be preserved as *her* birthplace. *(site 34)*

A painter almost from the time she had been old enough to hold a brush, Emily Carr was "discovered" in 1927 by a director of the National Gallery of Canada. Blooming under the warmth of praise from a national figure, she became Canada's most renowned female artist and the winner of the Governor General's award for her writing.

Although she travelled to San Francisco and later to England to study art and although she journeyed to coastal Indian villages and camped gypsy-style in forests to find subjects worthy of painting, Emily remained tied to the James Bay acres on which she was born. Richard Carr, who had been pre-deceased by his wife, died in 1888 when Emily was sixteen. He left his house and the land on which it sat to his children.

In 1913 Emily decided to build a small apartment house on her share of the property. Named Hill House because of its proximity to Beacon Hill Park, the house would become known as "The House of All Sorts" when Emily recounted her life as a landlady. *(site 36)*

EMILY CARR. *Between 1917 and 1921, Emily raised 350 sheepdogs in the back garden at Hill House.*

On her share of the estate, Emily's sister Alice, two years her senior built a small schoolhouse with modest living accommodations attached. In 1939 when seventy year old Alice had given up her school and was looking for a tenant to help defray the costs of operating the building, Emily announced that she was moving in.[28] After extensive alterations, which included painting her side of the schoolhouse's exterior and adapting the old schoolroom as a studio, Emily took up residence beside her sister who was somewhat bemused and far from pleased with the whirlwind changes Emily had wrought. *(site 35)*

Until Emily's death in 1945 the two sisters lived side-by-side, arguing, nagging and impatient with each other's foibles, but bound together by the affection of kinship and the loneliness of knowing that they were the last of Richard Carr's children to survive.

After Emily died, Alice who had never understood Emily's painting any more than she had understood Emily herself, suddenly felt a familial responsibility to honour her sister's memory. In 1946 she approached Victoria's city council. Would they, Alice asked allow her to erect a little bridge in Beacon Hill Park in her sister's name. Months and then years passed before the City made a decision. In 1953, after keeping the lonely, near blind old lady waiting for seven years, the city finally granted Alice's request. *(site 37)*

Colonist Feb.10'53
Tribute Paid Artist, Writer

ALICE CARR, Daily Colonist, February 10, 1953. Shortly before she died, Alice Carr attended the opening of her sister's bridge. Made of stones collected from the beach below Dallas Road, it carries a small plaque stating that it was erected in Emily's honour.

6.
"Agnes was very clever"

Like the Carrs, the Cameron family lived in James Bay and like Richard Carr, Duncan Cameron produced a daughter whose strength of will and ambition would bring her fame and brand her as eccentric.

Duncan Cameron was a Scot. He travelled to California during the 1850's and there he met Jessie Anderson, a native of Fifeshire who had gone to the Sacramento goldfields to keep house for her brother. Jessie and Duncan were married in California and three of their children were born there. Their fourth and last child, Agnes, was born in Victoria in 1863 shortly after

Cameron moved his family to the city.

"Agnes was very clever," Emily Carr remembered. At sixteen, when she had completed her formal education, Agnes received a teacher's certificate and began her career in the classrooms of Angela College, an Anglican girls' school on Burdett Street. (*site 54*) "Bouyant and vigorous," Agnes was a gifted teacher.

"School . . . became a delight rather than a drudgery, particularly when I passed into Miss Cameron's class," one of her students recalled.[29]

Agnes was too talented and too determined to be ignored. When she accepted a post at Victoria High School, she became the first woman to teach high school in British Columbia and when she was appointed principal of South Park School in her own James Bay neighbourhood, she became the province's first female school principal.

When Cameron died in 1912 at the age of forty-nine, testimonials to her influence appeared in papers throughout the province. "There is a legion of people . . . scattered over the world upon whom Death, in laying its remorseless hand on Agnes Deans Cameron, has inflicted a grievous personal loss," the *Victoria Times* intoned. "Upon them her remarkable personality and force of character created an impression so vivid that of all their school instructors she was the one who was best remembered."[30]

And it was true enough, for Agnes Cameron was not easy to forget. As well as being an extraordinarily able teacher, she was also bad tempered — an opinionated, argumentative woman who, only half in jest, posted a notice on her classroom door reading, "Irate parents received after 3 p.m."[31] She was incapable of compromise. Conciliation was foreign to her. During her teaching career, she moved from one confrontation to the next, taking on parents, principals, Superintendents and School Boards with equal enthusiasm. And on more than one occasion, she allowed her frustrations to explode in a rage directed at the handiest, rather than the most appropriate, victim.

On a March afternoon in 1890, Herbert Burkholder was sitting in Miss Cameron's geography class at the Victoria Boys' School. It was the fourth time he had attempted to master geography and his attention was flagging. Asked by Cameron to go to the wall map and point out the mountains of Europe, Herbert answered that he couldn't, he didn't know them.

"I told him that he should be able to answer such a simple question, that he must have learned it over and over," Cameron reported.[32]

After telling him to pay attention to the correct answer, she passed the question on to another student. Keep your eye on the wall map, she told Herbert.

Stung by the reprimand and annoyed that Cameron had called attention to the fact that he seemed to be permanently lodged in this geography class, Herbert quite deliberately turned his head the other way.

"I repeated my request once, twice, three times," Cameron reported.

"I'll learn it after school. I won't look at the map now," Herbert retorted.

Cameron was determined to emerge victorious from this battle of wills. It was, by her own account, only the second time in her ten-year teaching career that a student had refused to obey a direct order.

AGNES DEANS CAMERON.
*Precedent-setting and gifted, Agnes
was the first woman in British Columbia to teach high school and to serve
as a school principal.*

"Insubordination in the classroom," she said, "is like resisting an officer in the execution of his duty, or like mutiny on board a ship. It is a serious offense and must be promptly and decisively met."[33]

"I gave him two minutes to reverse his decision and then getting a whip, I told him I'd punish him until he changed his mind," Cameron recalled.

According to Cameron, Burkholder held out his hand two or three times and then bolted. Herbert's account was somewhat different. He had, he said, been severely beaten. Miss Cameron had struck him on the head and face.

Forced to refute Herbert's version of the events, Cameron amended her story. "I whipped him severely, just as severely as I possibly could," she admitted. "It is within range of possibility that in throwing up his arms to avoid punishment he may have been "touched" on the head, if so it was only a touch, and caused by the boy himself." And furthermore, Cameron continued, "Every stroke inflicted was a severe one and left a mark. If I had struck the boy on the head there would have been something left to show for it."[34]

For three days after his beating, Herbert played hooky. He refused to return to school. He would, he insisted, rather go to his grave than go to school. Parental pressure in the form of Mr. Burkholder changed his mind.

Poor Herbert! When he returned to school he was to find a punishment designed to cut more than any physical beating he had received. For Agnes Cameron was not interested in an apology. What she wanted and what she was determined to get, was abject surrender and complete submission.

When Mr. Burkholder and Herbert presented themselves at the door of Miss Cameron's classroom, she was sitting before a full assembly of his classmates. Prodded by his father, Herbert shuffled to her desk.

Was there a question she wanted to ask him, Herbert inquired, hoping perhaps that she would say, "Are you sorry, Herbert?" in which case he was prepared to gasp, "Yes, sorry," and escape to his desk.

"No," Cameron answered, she had no questions.

"Then, Herby," his father said from the doorway, "you may take your seat."

"Certainly not," Agnes thundered, "not while I am in charge of this room,

101

except by my permission.''

She would only take him back, she said, after he apologized for the trouble he had caused, promised implicit obedience in the future and agreed to submit quietly to any future punishment.

Herbert mumbled his apologies and humiliated and defeated he was allowed to return to class, to come to grips with important problems, like locating the mountains of Europe.

Agnes Cameron continued her teaching career until 1906 when she was fired by the Victoria School Board over the case of the South Park School drawing books. Students leaving junior schools were required to pass standardized examinations before being admitted to high schools. Drawing was one of the subjects examined. In 1905, the examination required students to complete perspective drawings of cubes, cones and cylinders. They were to be freehand sketches, teachers were warned. Straight-edges were not to be used.

When the South Park School drawing books were submitted to the Department of Education, it was discovered that most of the students' work showed evidence of rulers having been used. Cameron, it seemed, had ignored instructions. There was a chance that her students would be denied high school admission. Cameron could simply have claimed she hadn't read the instructions thoroughly. Or she could have said that she hadn't considered the use of a ruler an issue of great moment. Instead she flat-footedly denied that her students had used straight-edges and demanded a hearing before the Board. The trustees decided to establish a judicial enquiry.

For two months Judge Lampman pored over the drawing books and questioned all of Cameron's students. "We enjoyed showing our drawing books before the fatherly judge," Ada McGeer recalled.[35]

The judge's thirty-three page report concluded that rulers had been used by every student but one and Agnes Cameron's teaching career was over.[36]

AGNES DEANS CAMERON, *Mackenzie River, 1908. After her ten thousand mile journey around the Canadian north, Agnes worked up a series of lectures, with titles such as "Wheat, the Wizard of the North" and "Vancouver, Isle o' Dreams" and took her show on the road, spending two years in England on behalf of the Canadian government.*

Undaunted she threw herself into a new career as a travelling journalist and lecturer, appearing across North America and in England where her talks received enthusiastic reviews. When she returned to Victoria, she came as a celebrity.

When she died of pneumonia in 1912, four days after having undergone an appendix operation, she was remembered for her achievements rather than her cantankerousness. Her funeral was one of the largest Victoria had witnessed but the many floral wreaths sent to the family vault at Ross Bay Cemetery rested on an empty grave. For Agnes Cameron, resolutely opinionated to the end, had willed that she be cremated and her ungarlanded coffin sat at the Victoria docks awaiting transhipment to a Seattle crematorium.

7.
"John's Other Wife"

Innkeeper John Thomas Howard did not have a daughter who brought him fame. His fame, or notoriety, was due to the wives with which he was over-abundantly supplied.

After a sojourn in Australia, twenty-seven year old John Howard had returned to his native Manchester in 1851. He reacquainted himself with his aunt Mary McCandlish and her ten children. To all his stay-at-home McCandlish cousins, John must have appeared an adventurous and romantic figure but he singled out for special attention twenty-five year old Sarah, the oldest McCandlish daughter. She accepted his proposal even though she knew that their marriage would have to be postponed until John had found a position in life. He would go to the goldfields of California, he told her, and there he would make his fortune.

Unfortunately for Sarah, John delayed his departure for three years until 1854 and by then her sister Mary, who had been only fifteen when John first arrived, had bloomed into a fresh-faced eighteen and John found his attention diverted from the spinsterish, thirtyish Sarah.

On March 3, 1854 just days before his ship was due to sail, John and Mary were secretly married. The marriage was unconsummated.

"He left me the way he found me," Mary said.[37]

"I thought her the most virtuous woman in the world," John reported with some awe.[38]

And so John Howard set sail for California, leaving two McCandlish sisters, one to whom he was engaged and one to whom he was wed, patiently waiting for his return.

John spent the next four years in California. He had managed to grub together enough money to give him a start in business when he heard about the gold strikes on the Fraser River. He decided to move north into British territory. But first he sent for Mary.

In the only letter he had sent her way during his entire four year absence, he asked her to join him and enclosed his photograph together with $500 to pay for her passage. Mary's sister Sarah, by now aware of John's perfidy, intercepted his message. Without a word to Mary, she burned his letter, pocketed his $500 and tearing his photograph into pieces she returned it, with no explanation, to John.

John pronounced himself to be "quite cut up." But not, apparently, heartbroken. For it seems he had prepared for just such an eventuality by forming a liaison with another woman. She was Eleanor, "Nellie" to John, an Australian-born Irishwoman who had escaped from an unhappy marriage and was supporting herself in San Francisco as a washerwoman.

JOHN THOMAS HOWARD. *Unfortunately for John, he attended to his correspondence in the evening when he was "in his cups." Sober consideration might have suggested that he ignore the letter which brought his first wife within striking distance.*

She came to John "with all her clothes tied in a paper parcel" and together they travelled north to Vancouver Island. When they tumbled off the ship at Esquimalt, Howard recognized it as an admirable location for the saloon he intended to open.

For more than twenty years Nellie worked with John. She served as barmaid and when their saloon expanded into an inn, as cook and chambermaid. Since she and John had no children of their own, Nellie took into her care several young girls whose parents either couldn't or wouldn't look after them. In 1878 Nellie received the welcome news that her husband had drowned and since she was now free to marry, John took her "across the Sound" to Washington State for a marriage which Nellie believed to be completely legal, the anonymity of Washington necessary only because she and John had lived publicly together for so many years as man and wife.

Meanwhile, Mary McCandlish, John's legal wedded wife, had done her best to mend her wounded pride. In 1863 after waiting nine years to hear from John, she emigrated to Australia with her sisters. There she had married and had two children. When her husband died in 1879 she found herself almost penniless. It was then, as she contemplated the poverty of her future, that she began to think about John Howard.

When she tracked him down to Esquimalt and learned that he was a prosperous innkeeper and a well-known sportsman who associated with the "best people," she packed her bags, gathered up her two small children and set sail for Victoria.

John had learned that Mary had been making enquiries about him and when he heard she was ensconced in a Victoria hotel, he rushed to her, scrambling up the stairs in such haste that she heard his heavy breathing outside the door before he summoned the courage to knock.

"How he trembled," Mary noted with satisfaction. "He went down on his knees and asked me what I was going to do."[39]

He didn't get a straight answer from Mary, for she had, it seems, decided to keep her options open until she learned more about the financial and social position of her long-lost husband. She spent the next few days watching and listening. And receiving messages that were distinctly crossed.

He seemed well-off. "John's is the finest carriage in the place," she reported to Emma, her younger sister who had remained in Australia and who was consumed with curiosity about Mary's doings. But at the same time, Mary wrote, she had been warned that John was "such a liar that you cannot believe a word he says."

Adding to the difficulty of her decision were two proposals of marriage she received soon after her arrival. One was from the purser of the ship that had brought her from San Francisco. "Such a nice American," Mary mused, "younger a lot than John." The other was from a Cariboo-bound doctor, a "fine looking young fellow" who knew all about her situation but wanted to marry her anyway.

Within a week Mary had made her choice. "Oh Emma, I love him desperately." She would stay and exercise her legal claim to John. She now had to convince John to desert Nellie.

"She says she will not leave without a fight," Mary wrote. "I have seen her and she is *horrid*."

John made a feeble attempt to have the best of two worlds. "John begs me to go in a little house and he will come and see me. *Fancy that*," Mary gasped. Otherwise the fifty-seven year old innkeeper was quite content to enjoy witnessing the contest for which he was the prize.

Nellie having made it clear that she had no intention of giving up her man

MARY McCANDLISH. *Mary arrived in Victoria in the summer of 1881 bringing with her two small children, a particularly mean mind and more trouble for John Howard than he could have imagined possible.*

and her livelihood and fading discreetly away, Mary planned her campaign. Hoping to disgrace Nellie, she mulled over the idea of taking space in the newspaper to publicly proclaim her rival to be an adultress but she was forced to reconsider this plan of attack when it was pointed out to her that they had *all* been guilty of bigamy.

Fortunately for Mary she found an ally in the Church. An Anglican priest, after hearing Mary's story, decided that Nellie must be expelled from the Communion table.

"Fancy her taking the Sacrament," Mary mewed.

He marched into the Howards' inn and delivered his verdict, leaving Nellie so distraught that she took the unprecedented step of closing the bar. Faced with the shame of church expulsion, she agreed to leave John, provided that he give her enough money to allow her to buy a boarding house.

On August 18, 1881 Mary wrote exultantly to Emma. "I am indeed with my darling John. He came for me in the evening driving me himself, such a glorious moonlight night. I was just the happiest wife in the world and hope we may both live to be ninety. What a kind good tempered easily pleased lover he is."

The honeymoon was soon over. Nellie, "that impudent Irish thing," continued to call herself "Mrs Howard" and, Mary reported, "In a great many people's eyes I am just as bad as she is."

John had had to mortgage the inn to pay Nellie off. "I have worked like a nigger since I came here," Mary grumbled. "I work all the time."

Six months after she moved in with John, Mary made a most extraordinary suggestion to her unmarried sister. First she reminded Emma of the time that an Australian, who she referred to as "old Leathercheeks" had proposed to Emma. Was she going to marry him? Mary had asked. And Emma had retorted that she would marry him if Mary would sleep with him. Now Mary had a similar idea in mind.

EMMA McCANDLISH. *Cunningly disguised as the* Daily Colonist, *Emma is prepared for one of the many parties enlivened by her presence.*

'I am going to make you an offer,'' she wrote, ''and I can certify to the great kindness you would receive from John. You see, dear, he tells me pretty often I am spoiled — that's the worst of it — so if you could come and take my place in that sense, he could not say that of you and it would make matters right. I told John I would tell you this so leave it for your consideration.''

Just how seriously forty year old Emma considered this offer is unknown, but if she wasn't inflamed by passion, she was certainly burning with curiosity and within a few months she had arrived in Victoria.

Emma never married. For a time she worked as a housekeeper and then, using a small inheritance, she set up a boarding house on Superior Street behind the Parliament Buildings. Enjoying a robust constitution, she celebrated her seventy-fifth birthday by attending a ball at which she was described as being ''one of the gayest and most lighthearted of the guests.'' She died in 1921 in her eightieth year, proud that just months before she had danced at a ball at the Empress Hotel given in honour of the Prince of Wales.

In 1887 John Howard suffered a stroke which left him paralyzed and unable to speak. He lingered on for eight years, cared for by Mary, who, one suspects, may have been a less than solicitous nurse.

Nellie Howard opened a boarding house in Victoria and spent the last years of her life cared for with love and gratitude by one of her adopted daughters, Florrie Nunn, who had married the province's premier architect, Francis Mawson Rattenbury.

V. Victoria's Heyday

1.
"good, heavy and substantial"

In 1880 a visitor from New York arrived in Victoria and recorded his impressions.[1] "Here one has neither the evening winds and disagreeable fogs of San Francisco, nor the rather noxious breezes and mosquitoes of Portland, Oregon. The skies are ever clear, the air is always refreshingly cool, the people look quiet and respectable, and everything is intensely English." It was enough to swell Victorians' hearts with civic pride until they read on and discovered what constituted this American's definition of Englishness.

"Everything is good, heavy, and substantial — the people, the buildings, the food, the drinks," he wrote. And then with the sang-froid of a man who was not planning to return, he continued, "The girls even, as compared with the beauties of San Francisco, tend towards the ponderous . . .""

Victorians may have been slightly rattled by this characterization of the female population but they must have been rather pleased that he had noted the good, solid and substantial appearance of the town.

The population boom Victoria experienced during the 1880's — a steady, almost predictable growth of one thousand a year — had begun to change the look of the city. One by one the tired, wooden gold rush buildings were disappearing and in their place stout brick business blocks were creating a mood of permanence and stability.

The Theatre Royal on Government Street, scene of the race riot more than twenty years earlier, was demolished in 1882. Two years later Morley's Soda Water Factory, housed in a handsome two story brick building costing $6000, replaced some of the old redwood buildings Waddington had built along his

VICTORIA OPERA HOUSE, DRIARD HOTEL. *Built in 1885 and now housing Eaton's department store, the hotel was entered from Douglas Street, the theatre from View.*

alley in 1858. (*site 25*) In 1882 a fire destroyed the Driard's mansard roof. As renovations began, it was decided to combine the hotel's reconstruction with a proposed opera house. By 1885 the Driard was presenting a crisp new face along Douglas Street and around the corner on View, the Victoria Opera House had opened, its financial position secured by the hundred hotel rooms that had been built above it. (*site 20*)

In 1885 the Union Club, a private gentleman's club patterned on the English model and presided over by Sir Matthew Baillie Begbie, moved from its rented rooms above Van Volkenberg's butcher shop into a new clubhouse at the corner of Douglas and Courtney. Costing $16,000 the Club's new home was described as the "finest and costliest" building built during the year.

Residential construction kept pace with the growing population. In the Spring Ridge area and on the Work estate dozens of Queen Anne cottages, costing between $600 and $2500 and painted in "lively and harmonious" colours were built. Larger, more expensive homes, costing as much as $6000, were appearing in James Bay and along Johnson, Fort and other streets which ran eastward from town.

By 1889, 'Craigdarroch Castle', the single most spectacular addition to the cityscape that the decade would see, was nearing completion. (*site 43*) With an estimated cost of half a million dollars, 'Craigdarroch' was the most expensive residence in the province. A dream-castle, a fantasy of soaring chimneys, towers and turrets, steeply-pitched red-tiled gables and exquisitely crafted stained glass windows, the castle was finished with the best materials the richest man in British Columbia could find.

By 1889 Victoria was well on its way to becoming a city of beautiful houses,

'CRAIGDARROCH CASTLE', *1050 Joan Crescent. Built on twenty-eight acres of the highest point of land in the city, 'Craigdarroch' was designed by architects Smith and Williams of Portland, Oregon.*

'TREBATHA', *1124 Fort Street. Fort Street continued to be fashionable during the 1880's when Dr. T.J. Jones, first president of the B.C. Dental Association, spent $8000 to build 'Trebatha'.*

a garden city and "one of the prettiest on the continent." But it was also a manufacturing center with the largest iron-works on the Pacific coast outside San Francisco, with five boot and shoe factories, four wagon and carriage factories, a saw mill, a planing mill, a box factory, a meat packing house, half a dozen cigar factories, two book binderies, two soap works, two cracker bakeries and a corset factory.

Victorians could take pride in the fact that they lived in the largest and wealthiest city in the province.

2.
"most pleasing and pretty"

During the 1880's Victoria took several giant steps toward the twentieth century. The Esquimalt and Nanaimo Railway arrived in town. Electric lighting was introduced. Free home delivery of mail was initiated. A sewage system was finally begun. And a street railway system opened the suburbs to development.

A condition of British Columbia's entry into Confederation had been the construction of a transcontinental rail line which would link the Pacific coast with the Canadian provinces in the east. Victorians presumed that their city, as the provincial capital, would become the railroad's western terminus. But early in 1880, the northerly route which would have brought the line across island bridges to Nanaimo and down to Victoria was rejected. Instead the tracks would end at Burrard Inlet. The decision resulted in a mainland boom. "Gastown" would become Vancouver and Vancouver would become the center of commerce and would replace Victoria as the province's largest city.

Victorians were dismayed when they learned of the decision, particularly so since the man who made it, Prime Minister Sir John A. Macdonald, sat in the federal House as the Member of Parliament for Victoria. In an attempt to placate Islanders, the federal government agreed to finance the construction of a rail line between Nanaimo and Victoria, which would be linked to the terminus of the main line by a fleet of steamers.

Construction of the Esquimalt and Nanaimo Railway began in 1884 and two years later the line was complete, its final golden spike hammered home by Prime Minister Macdonald at Cliffside near Shawnigan Lake. At first the tracks had ended at Esquimalt, but Victorians, particularly those who owned downtown property, succeeded in having the tracks extended across the bridge at the foot of Johnson Street into the heart of the business district. On March 29, 1888 a civic holiday was declared and a happy crowd of Victorians gathered to toss their hats in the air as the first train eased into its Store Street terminal. (*site 27*)

Victoria's city council had become less than sanguine about the cost and quality of the street lighting provided by the gas company. When Robert Burns McMicking suggested that he could light the city by electricity for $6000 a year, he received an eager response.

McMicking had already proved that he was adept at recognizing the value of new technology. In 1878, just two years after the device was patented, he obtained the agency for the Bell telephone in Victoria. He ordered two telephones, shipped from Chicago, and on March 21, 1878 he demonstrated them to an impressed reporter from the *Colonist* who gasped, "People standing fifteen miles apart can hear each other speak." The *Colonist* became one of McMicking's first subscribers and by 1880 the directory included forty-six numbers, ten of them assigned to residences.[2]

McMicking's proposal, approved by the ratepayers on July 25, 1883, called for the erection of three tall light poles, one at the corner of Yates and Government, another at Blanshard and Chatham and the third below Church Hill near the intersection of Blanshard and Burdett. Each pole would be topped with a 50,000 candle-power arc light. On the night of December 21, 1883, council members assembled to test the new lighting system. They walked to the corner of Blanshard and Fisgard, observed that "ordinary type could be plainly read," and hied themselves back to city hall to ratify McMicking's contract and to cancel the city's agreement with the gas company.

The experiment proved so successful that in 1885 the city voted to install twenty-one lamps of 2000 candle power in the business district. By 1889 the city was bathed in light.

"Looking down from an eminence the electric lights scattered over the city — the mast lights standing high and throwing out dazzling rays for long distances, the single lights making bright the dark streets — the effect is most pleasing and pretty," the *Colonist* enthused.[3]

The carbons in the arc lamps atop their 160-foot-high masts had to be cleaned every day and McMicking was fortunate to find in his employ a man for whom heights presented no problem. Born in Scotland in 1852, Andrew Gibson had served aboard clipper ships on the China sea trade. "We used to take in sail only when they had begun to blow away," Gibson recalled.[4] To a man who had scrambled up the spars during dirty weather off the Horn and the Cape when he was seventeen years old, climbing Victoria's lighting masts was child's play. But on one occasion, at least, child's play turned life threatening.

A winter's gale blew out the lights on the mast near Church Hill. Drenched with wind-whipped rain, Andrew Gibson climbed the mast and fixed the carbons. When he tried to descend, he discovered that his scaling ropes had fouled. Far below him, he heard footsteps. Hailing the man, Gibson clung to his perch as the passer-by tried unsuccessfully to untangle the ropes. As Gibson's supply of salty language was near exhaustion, another, more dextrous pedestrian arrived to rescue him and the first man on the scene, who Gibson would later learn had been the Anglican bishop, wandered away shaking his head and murmuring, "I am sorry for that man up there but I am bound to say he can outswear any man I ever heard."

LIGHT TOWER, *corner of Blanshard and Burdett Streets. Probably taken from Christ Church Cathedral, which stood on the site now occupied by the Law Courts, this photograph shows the Inner Harbour from Laurel Point on the right, to the James Bay bridge and the mud-flats.*

In fair weather and foul, Gibson ensured that Victoria was well lit. Daily he scaled the Douglas fir masts — one hundred feet to the cross trees and sixty feet to the lamps above. His little buggy was pulled by Kitty, a city-owned horse who knew his route as well as he did.

"She'd start up when she saw I was through with one lamp and go right along to the next and stop there," Gibson said. "The kiddies all knew her and me, and they'd follow us to get the old carbons from me to use for crayons."

For eighteen years Gibson and Kitty were partners. When she became supernumerary, Gibson, afraid that the city would sell her off, smuggled her away to a farm in Saanich. "I used to go out and visit her," he remembered. "She lived in peace and quietness a year or two and then she died. Kitty and me, we were great chums."

3.
"busy metropolitan style"

On Dominion Day, 1888 the federal government announced that it would celebrate Canada's birthday by giving its most western capital a present. Beginning on July 3, mail would be delivered without charge to all residents who informed the postmaster in advance in writing that they wanted the service. The city was divided into four postmen's walks. Letters would be delivered twice a day. And even though the city housed no more than 12,000 individuals, it does seem that the post office was expecting rather a lot from the four mail carriers it hired to accomplish the task.[5]

It was ironic that just as the post office adopted a policy which would relieve Victorians of the necessity of making the trek into town to collect their mail, a private company was taking steps to make it much easier for them to get there.

One of the reasons that Victoria's boundaries had not expanded and that close-to-town James Bay properties had been subdivided into smaller and smaller lots was the difficulty of getting around. Walking was one solution. But even though some might find the three mile hike to Oak Bay no more than a pleasant stroll, it wasn't necessarily a trip one would want to make every day. Residents who owned a field and a barn kept a horse and buggy, either an English dogcart, high and two-wheeled and with the driver sitting "two cushions higher" than the passengers and with his cracking whip whistling dangerously close to his lady-passenger's hats or an American buggy with a hood that could be folded up or down like a baby's pram. For special trips, the town's livery stables rented horses or provided hacks — the boxy, stuffy carriages that came with a driver and could be rented for excursions to the

BRAY'S LIVERY STABLE. *Open carriages carrying up to twelve passengers could be rented for trips to Esquimalt and Saanich.*

countryside. Weary businessmen or parcel-laden shoppers could collect a ride in one of the hacks that waited in a patient row along Government Street outside the post office.

HACKS, *Government Street. Hacks waited for passengers along Government Street in front of the Italianate post office built in 1873.*

"There was very seldom a cabbie in sight there," one hack-rider recalled. "You had to go into the nearest pub to retrieve him. They put in hours of waiting for fares and they killed time by going into the nearest pub . . . there was a bar on every corner and very often in between."[6]

In 1883 Francis Stilman Barnard decided to take a leaf out of his father's book. Francis Jones Barnard had founded the Cariboo Express, the famous "B.X." that had jolted along the Cariboo Wagon Road carrying supplies from Yale to Barkerville. In January, 1883 his son formed the Victoria Transfer Company. Barnard had ambitious plans. More than simply adding to the stock of horses and hacks for hire, he intended to establish an omnibus service, a fleet of large, horse-drawn carriages which would travel through the city along specified routes and at regular intervals.

In 1885 Barnard built a large stable on Broughton Street at Broad to house the sixty horses, twelve hacks, thirty buggies and eight omnibuses his company had acquired. And in November he announced the beginning of the company's 'bus service. Between the hours of 8 a.m. and 8 p.m. and for a fare of 10 cents, passengers could travel along either of two routes: from Fort and Yates Streets to the Point Ellice Bridge; and from Hillside and Douglas through James Bay to the Outer Wharf.[7]

The popularity of the omnibuses encouraged others to enter the transportation field. In October, 1888 the National Electric Tramway and Lighting Company received council's permission to lay track, erect poles and run electrically-powered tram-cars along city streets. Construction began the following June and the street railway system was formally opened on February 22, 1890 with two hundred "prominent gentlemen" gathering at the company's Rock Bay power house to drink champagne, to crowd aboard the company's four-car fleet and to speed through town at 10 miles an hour in "busy metropolitan style."

The service was an instant success. By the end of the year, the company's president, David Higgins, former editor of the *Colonist* reported that the street-cars were carrying some 2000 passengers a month.[8]

Soon residents and real estate speculators were clamoring for additions to the first two routes which followed the paths established by the omnibuses and the line to Esquimalt which had been added in October, 1890.

"I am constantly besieged with applications for extensions," Higgins announced with some satisfaction.

FORT STREET CAR. *The company policy which prohibited smoking inside the cars resulted in rear platforms heavy with nicotine-dependent gentlemen. "It is quite a common thing to see men, and even ladies, elbowing their way through the crowd on the platform in order to get access to the car," a passenger complained.*

The land speculators who formed the Oak Bay Land and Improvement Company and who had noted a rival developer advertising his lots near the Jubilee Hospital as being "eight minutes by electric cars from the post office," proposed the laying of tracks to the beach at Oak Bay. The Tramway Company, having learned something from the concession-grabbing tactics adopted by the Canadian Pacific Railway, responded that they might consider such a move if the development company paid a $15,000 subsidy and if they received a gift of 25 acres of land along the route.[9] Waiting in line behind the Oak Bay developers was the B.C. Agricultural Association which ran the fairgrounds at the "Willows" and which was convinced that an extension of the tracks would increase attendance at its annual exhibition and the horse races and other events staged at the six-acre grounds.

WILLOWS FAIRGROUND. *Built in 1891 for $45,000
and completed in sixty-five days, the exhibition hall was
located just north of Fair Street between Henderson and
Cadboro Bay Roads.*

By the end of 1891 negotiations had been successfully concluded. The Fort
Street line had been extended past the Royal Jubilee Hospital at Richmond
Road to the doorstep of the Willows Hotel on Cadboro Bay Road just a
minute's walk from the fairground. And a shuttle service had been established
between Fort Street and the beach at Oak Bay.

Land speculators were well aware that a street-car line increased the value
of their holdings and boomlets of development followed the route of each
new line. But the Tramway Company was too canny to rely only on com-
muters for custom. If no particular attraction existed at the end of a route,
they took steps to create one. The events that took place at the Willows and
at Beacon Hill Park, to which a line began running in 1892, provided ready-
made lures. But, the company thought, the beach at Oak Bay, although it
was a popular summer-destination and the site of the magnificent Mount
Baker Hotel, could do with some improvement. In 1895, on eleven beach-
side acres, the company began work on the Oak Bay Recreation Park which
would include a bicycle track and a 2000-seat grandstand and would provide
"first class facilities for all kinds of out-door sports."[10]

Whatever its ultimate attractions, the Oak Bay route was not without its
problems. Passing through open countryside, the line was often blocked by
wandering cows. Derailments were common, caused, the company said, by
small boys who put rocks on the track, but more likely due to the fact that
the new cars ordered were of a slightly different gauge to the original cars
and didn't quite fit the tracks.[11] But the problems encountered on the Oak
Bay route were nothing compared to those experienced on the Esquimalt run,
heavily patronized by off-duty sailors.

One night passengers aboard the Esquimalt car outbound from Victoria
were startled by an "awful racket" coming from the roof of the car. "There

was a concertina playing and a thumping of feet,'' a passenger recalled. The car was immediately stopped and the motorman and conductor scrambled out to discover half-a-dozen sailors who had remained perfectly quiet until they decided that the time was right for startling the passengers by beginning their jig. "It took an awful lot of arguing, but we got them down."[12]

CAR NUMBER TWO, *Esquimalt Line*.

There were times when the proximity of the naval base was a distinct advantage. If a car carrying a contingent of sailors derailed, the "bluejackets" hopped out, lifted the car up and placed it back on the tracks. Even if no naval men were aboard, their assistance was never far away. An English visitor aboard the Esquimalt car became incensed when, after his car derailed, the conductor simply glanced at his watch and then settled himself down for a companionable chat with the motorman. In answer to the visitor's complaints, the conductor patiently explained that they would be back on the tracks and on their way in twenty minutes. Before the time was up a naval physical training squad panted into view. They hoisted the car onto the tracks and then smartly jogged off continuing their morning work-out.[13]

Between 1881 and 1891, the city's population grew by more than 10,000, from 5,925 to 16,841, and as the city grew so did the problems of sewage disposal. Solid waste was deposited in privies, box-like contraptions which were stored outside and which were emptied after midnight by scavengers. Undesirable as it may have been in town, human waste was welcomed by the Chinese market gardeners who supplied the city with fresh vegetables from their gardens in the Fairfield estate above Dallas Road between Moss and Cook Streets. "Night-soil", obtained from the scavengers, steamed in cesspools sited here and there in the gardens and when it had reached the consistency of "liquid manure" it was spread on the lettuce and celery which would be eaten a few weeks later in the best houses in Victoria. As Victoria became more urban, the practice began to meet with opposition and a wharf was built at Ross Bay from which night-soil was deposited directly into the sea and from where it promptly washed back onto the beach.

Adding to the public's growing distaste was the transportation of sewage through city streets. "The Scavengers could not start collecting till after midnight," a resident recalled, "but it was a very nasty experience when returning from a late dance, or a Ball, accompanied by ladies, to encounter a row of 'night-soil' laden tumbrels with their odoriferous contents."[14]

Obviously something had to be done and in 1890 construction began on a sewage system which would move effluent through the city below ground and which would deposit its load further out to sea at the tip of Clover Point.

Construction was well underway by October, 1891 when Augustus Pemberton lay dying at 'Glenville', his home perched on the rocks above Clover Point. For his son Chartres, who kept watch over his father from midnight to dawn, the construction of the sewer and his father's death would remain bound together in his memory. The contractors were running a tunnel down Moss Street to Clover Point, Pemberton recalled. At the corner of May and Moss Streets, the water that collected in the tunnel was pumped out of a well and into a stream that ran into Ross Bay. During the long nights, sitting alone beside his father's bed, Pemberton listened for the pump to start up when the well became full. It was the only company he had and the only distraction he allowed himself.

"The stillness of the night watch was interrupted regularly every twenty-five minutes by the busy little pump," Pemberton would recall years later.

The thirty-five years that had passed since Augustus Pemberton had begun homesteading in the wild countryside of Fairfield and Oak Bay had brought many changes. The little farming community, centered on a fur trade fort, which had boomed into a gold town was now well on its way to becoming a sophisticated city, a "stately capitol", which would act like a magnet, pulling people out of the Prairies and Eastern Canada, drawing them from England and from the colonial outposts of India, Singapore and Hong Kong. Over the next twenty-three years, from 1891 till the outbreak of the Great War, Victoria would experience its heyday.

4.
"Nearly Two Millions!"

Well-lit and soon to be well-plumbed, with telephones, mail delivery and an expanding street-car service, Victoria entered the 1890's with confidence and optimism.

"Nearly Two Millions!" the *Colonist* headlined a special New Years Day edition which detailed the value of construction projects undertaken in 1890.

Thirty business blocks had been erected in town. "A few years ago a two story brick store was considered quite good enough for Victoria; now three, four and five-story blocks of brick and stone are needed to meet the necessities of the day.''

Outside the business district four hundred houses had been completed in 1890. James Bay was considered to be "almost completely filled". Spring Ridge and the Work estate were "rapidly building up" and Victoria West had become "a town in itself."

Rockland Avenue, still inelegantly known as Belcher Street, was coming into its own as the residential street favoured by the rich. Curving and winding with the lay of the land, Belcher Street so appealed to businessman Robert Ward that when rising fortune suggested he build a new house, he moved the three-gabled gothic cottage in which he had been living down the hill to Richardson Street and built his new residence on the site it had occupied. (*sites 48, 49*)

The 'Laurels', designed by architect Thomas Sorby and costing $27,000, was completed in November, 1890 and drew raves for its Moorish window, its huge entrance hall with ceiling twenty-seven feet high, its alcoves and inglenooks and bay windows, and sixty feet above the lawn, its combined observatory-smoking room. But however grand the 'Laurels', it ranked only second to 'Gisburn'.

'GISBURN'. *'Gisburn' was demolished in the 1940's and its grounds were sub-divided into small residential lots.*

A short distance along Belcher Street, 'Gisburn' was set in manicured grounds surrounded by a stone wall. With its name carved into its gate-posts (*site 47*), 'Gisburn' was not only imposing but also whimsically colourful. At least five different colours and shades of colour had been used to pick out the decorative features on Gisburn's cupola and around each of its many doors and windows and to define the five differently shaped bands of shingles which wound around its roof.

Years after it had been discovered by the O'Reillys, the Gorge was rivalling the Rockland area as the neighbourhood favoured by mansion-builders. Here residents could enjoy picturesque waterfront properties protected from the spray-filled gales that occasionally rocked the houses along Dallas and Esquimalt Roads. In 1890, Andrew Gray, manager of the Albion Iron Works, made a relatively modest addition to the neighbourhood when he spent $9000 to build 'Roslyn', a delicate Queen Anne house, sited so as to present its best side to the water, the direction from which many guests would arrive. (*site 56*)

'ROSLYN', *1135 Catherine Street.*
When 'Roslyn' served as a film set,
Bruce Dern was required to leap from
its second floor balcony.

By more than $20,000 the largest residential project undertaken in 1890 was the $53,000 Joan Dunsmuir spent adding finishing touches to 'Craigdarroch'. But then the Dunsmuirs really were in a class by themselves.

In 1850, Robert Dunsmuir, a twenty-five year old Ayrshire coal-miner, had signed a contract with the HBC to work the Company's coal mines on the north-east coast of the Island. In 1869, working on his own behalf, he discovered the Wellington Seam, the richest coal deposit on Vancouver Island. His start-up operations funded by naval officers, in 1883 Dunsmuir was able to buy out the last remaining partner for $600,000. The same year he moved from Nanaimo to Victoria, where he bought and enlarged 'Fairview' across Menzies Street from the 'Birdcages' in James Bay, where he lived while he sought out the best building site in the city for the construction of his castle.

Robert Dunsmuir died in 1889, before 'Craigdarroch' was completed. His wife Joan moved into the castle a very rich widow, for Robert's simple one page will had named her his only beneficiary. Controlling the family commercial empire, she also controlled her children. Her sons, James and Alexander, both in their thirties when their father died, continued to work for their mother, aware that at any time Joan could cut them out of the family fortune.

Joan's disapproval prevented Alexander, who managed the company's coal sales in San Francisco, from marrying the woman with whom he had been living for many years and the stress of his tangled domestic life may have contributed to his abuse of alcohol which killed him when he was forty-six, within weeks of having made an honest woman of his cohabitant.

James Dunsmuir, safely married when his father died and well on the way to producing a family of eight daughters and two sons, had found his position less tenuous than Alexander's. He moved from Nanaimo to Victoria to take over Robert's management role and in 1892 built a palatial home on the banks of the Gorge. Designed by architect John Teague and built for an estimated cost of between $30,000 and $50,000, 'Burleith' was a showplace, set in twenty acres of tennis courts, croquet lawns and bridal paths.

'BURLEITH.' *James Dunsmuir's Gorge-side home was destroyed by fire in 1931. Part of the stone wall that surrounded the estate can be seen along Craigflower Road.*

James was tortured by the thought that while he and his brother worked long hours to maximize the company's profits, Joan would use the income they produced to acquire for her unmarried daughters the best houses and the best husbands that money could buy. For a reminder of Joan's earlier munificence, James had only to look across the waters of the Gorge to see the towers of 'Ashnola', the grand home occupied by his sister Emily and her husband Northing Pinkney Snowden whose contribution to the family assets seems to have ended with his name. On the Esquimalt waterfront another sister, Mary, was the mistress of 'Mount Adelaide' and while her husband Henry Croft, a mill owner after whom the town of Crofton was named, was at least self-supporting, the title to 'Mount Adelaide' was in Joan Dunsmuir's name.

Eventually the family tensions created by Robert's will and by James' distaste for most of his brothers-in-law would bring the Dunsmuirs into court, the possession of the family fortune settled only after a series of hearings as lengthy as the evidence submitted was bizarre. But during the 1890's an uneasy peace continued and the members of the Dunsmuir family, so rich that their humble beginnings could be overlooked, if not forgotten, took their place as the leaders of society.

'ASHNOLA'. *Built in 1889 for $25,000, 'Ashnola' stood across the water from 'Burleith'.*

In 1887 Charlotte Doane explained the social facts of life to Florence Baillie-Grohman. Florence had recently arrived from England and as her husband was planning to spend some months on the mainland she had been looking for a place to stay. Charlotte, who lived alone with her daughter in a large house, had been persuaded to let her use two otherwise unoccupied rooms.

Florence seems to have needed no instruction on the social niceties, for as the daughter of a Master of Hounds and the wife of a well-known sports man who had decided to invest some of his capital canal-building in the Kootenays, her name had soon appeared on the guest lists of the best houses in town and Sir Matthew Baillie Begbie and a string of Pembertons, Creases and Tyrwhitt-Drakes had begun appearing on Mrs Doane's doorstep, to call on Florence. But not on Mrs Doane.

"She was not at all popular in Victoria as she had what people would vulgarly call 'no class'," Florence reported. [16]

One of the eighteen children born to Irish parents, Charlotte had immigrated to Australia. There she had received a letter from a brother in California saying that he had struck it rich and asking her to come to San Francisco to keep house for him. When she reached San Francisco, she learned that her brother had been shot in "a card affray." Presented with two bags of gold that represented her brother's estate, Charlotte had been wondering what to do next when Joseph Homer Doane, the captain of the ship that had brought her to California, proposed to her. She spent the next few years sailing up and down the coasts of North America in her husband's ship.

When Captain Doane sailed into Victoria in 1858, he decided to leave the sea and invest in town lots. In 1872 when other investors were still pinched by the depression, he discovered that he had received a legacy of £ 74,000 or about $370,000.[17] Captain Doane died in 1883 leaving Charlotte with strategically located downtown properties and the capital to develop them however she wished.

But Mrs Doane's money hadn't bought her a place in society and she retaliated by telling Florence all she knew about the families who considered her not worth knowing.

"She knew the history of everyone in the town," Florence said. "She would sometimes say of someone, with a sneer, perhaps a smart lady in society, 'Who is she? Why her father had only got a second rate schooner. Of course it was easy for her to marry her man because there were so few white women here then." And, Florence, continued, "There were many . . . whom she knew had Indian forbears."

Most Victorians probably knew everything about Mrs Doane's background too, for she was nothing if not voluble. And after the Chief of Police presented a "confidential" report to David Higgins and the other members of the City's police committee, many may have learned that Charlotte Doane owned the Broad Street buildings out of which operated Nettie, Mable, Jennie and Louisa — four of the town's most successful madams.[18]

The chief's report, prepared in 1886, listed a total of fourteen houses of prostitution, run by madams and containing thirty-eight girls. Most of them were on Broad and Broughton Streets, conveniently close to the Driard and one of them, according to rumour, directly connected by a tunnel with the new Douglas Street premises of the Union Club. A total of fifty-two prostitutes might have seemed an ample supply. But, the report continued, this number only included the white practitioners. On Fisgard Street, the chief estimated, more than 100 Chinese women plied the trade.

5.
"celestials"

It was not surprising that the chief had only been able to come up with an estimate of the number of Chinese prostitutes for Chinatown kept its secrets from census takers, tax collectors and police constables alike. Covering the area between Pandora, Government, Store and Herald and spilling over to the adjacent streets, Chinatown, behind the bland facade it presented to the non-Oriental, was a maze of interconnecting narrow alleyways and hidden inner courtyards. (*site 28*) The real life of the community took place within this secret city, screened from prying eyes and safe from the taunts and jibes that were often experienced on the streets.

PANDORA STREET, *during the 1880's. The space between the wooden balconies marks the entrance to Fan Tan Alley.*

The first Chinese had arrived in Victoria from San Francisco in 1858 and since most of them went directly to the Fraser, their presence had caused not the slightest ripple of excitement. But by 1860 they had begun to trickle back to Victoria from the mines and others had arrived from China and their increasing numbers began to have an impact of public attitudes. At a meeting held to discuss ways of increasing the colonial revenues, it was suggested that a head tax be collected from every Chinese entering the colony. Alfred Waddington, the man who had condemned injustices to Indians, supported the idea. He disapproved of the coming of the Chinese, Waddington said. They produced nothing and simply wanted to mine as much gold as possible and leave.[19] The proposal was defeated partly because some agreed with architect John Wright's contention that it was unfair to single out the Chinese, but mostly because it was recognized that such a move might be bad for business.

During the 1860's most Victorians continued to view Chinese residents with a superior air of patronizing and amused detachment typified by the *Colonist's* whimsical account of the haunting of a house in 1867. "The Chinese servant reports that he has heard strange noises, footsteps, groans and knockings," the paper reported. "One occasion a lighted candle he held in his hand was blown out by some invisible agency. John's pigtail has stood on end ever since . . . and when he leaves the house on an errand he puts his hat on the point of the tail instead of his head."

Basically incurious, Victorians failed to realize that the Chinese who were settling in Victoria fell into two distinct groups: a small, educated commercial class of merchants who were prepared to take an active and equal role in the community, and a larger class of agricultural workers who in their home provinces in China had been among the poorest.

No matter that by the summer of 1862 the Kwong Lee Company "Importers and Dealers in all kinds of Chinese Goods, Rice, Sugar, Tea, Provisions" was doing more trade than any other business in town with the exception of the HBC,[20] Victorians continued to view the "celestials" as primitive and child-like and objects of fun.

Matters did not improve during the 1880's when the Canadian Pacific Railway made agreements with Chinese labour contractors to import thousands of "Johns" to clear the railroad's main line. Nor did Robert Dunsmuir improved the situation when he hired Chinese strike-breakers to work in his coal mines. Anti-Oriental agitation began when white workingmen perceived the Chinese as a huge docile workforce prepared to work for less and under less favourable conditions than their white counterparts. By 1884 anti-Chinese sentiments had reached such a fever pitch that the federal government appointed a Commission on Chinese Immigration to investigate the issue.

During the commissioners' visit to Victoria, the police chief escorted them through Chinatown to inspect opium dens, apparently with the purpose of providing proof of depravity. But to the surprise of both the chief and the commissioners, they encountered several white men indulging in a pipe among their fellow addicts. And even more surprisingly, they happened upon Emily Wharton, a twenty-two year old prostitute from San Francisco who frankly admitted that she had been smoking opium for four years, that she found it much less harmful than alcohol and that she had never been subjected to any untoward behavior in this or any other opium den.[21]

So rivetting did the commissioners find Emily and her defense of opium that it seems they gave very little thought to recommending its prohibition and opium continued to be manufactured, sold and smoked openly in Chinatown until its possession was banned by federal law in 1908. In 1889 Victoria's City Directory listed fourteen opium factories and Victorians became familiar with the odour produced during the drug's manufacture. "You could smell it all over Victoria — the odour was very much like boiling potatoes."[22]

Despite impassioned testimony in its favour, the proposal to exclude the further immigration of Orientals did not win favour with the commissioners. Instead they suggested that immigration be controlled by taxing every Chinese entering the country. In 1885 the federal government instituted a fifty dollar head tax — providing an incentive for the illegal smuggling of Chinese into the country and for the construction of passageways which interconnected Chinatown buildings on their upper floors allowing a person, pursued by the police, to enter one building and emerge from another half a block away.

During the commission's hearings, the Chinese had not been without their defenders, men characterized by leading anti-Orientalist Arthur Bunster, a Victoria brewer, as "would-be aristocrats who like to put on frills and are fond of having Chinese servants."[23] Fitting that description was Henry Pelling Perew Crease, a Supreme Court judge and the owner of 'Pentrelew', a stately home on Fort Street. Arguing against any policy of Chinese exclusion, Crease warned, "The wail of the housewife would sweep through the land, and find a very decided expression in every husband's vote at the polls."[24]

Crease knew whereof he spoke. Without the Chinese the servant problem would have been acute. Domestics recruited in England could be counted on to work for only a few weeks. "No sooner does an unmarried woman arrive here than a host of admirers offer to make her happy for life," the *Colonist* noted in 1861. Ladies discovered to their delight that, given the proper training, a Chinese servant was an improvement over the average English cook or housemaid. "He does twice the work, he is far more cleanly in his manner of doing it, he is always sober, and fairly honest," one enthusiast raved.[25] And soon every house of any pretension had a "Chinaman's room", either in the bowels of the basement or tucked off the kitchen scullery.

BACHELORS' QUARTERS, *Chinatown. Not all Chinese who worked as cooks, houseboys or gardeners used the "Chinaman's Room". Most returned to Chinatown for the night, where they lived in tenement buildings sharing rooms heated by small woodstoves.*

When Florence Baillie-Grohman rented a small house on Douglas Street she had been pleasantly surprised to learn that eighteen year old Gee came with it. She came to depend on Gee's efficient management of the house; as she settled herself into Victoria's society, she gradually came to realize that some of the city's social conventions had been shaped by Chinese servants rather than their mistresses.

"On Sunday afternoon," Florence wrote, "every household is emptied of its Chinamen, for they all expect a half day off, and leaving as soon as the mid-day meal is cleared away, often refuse to come back and get the supper, and do not appear again until Monday morning."[26]

Knowing that the lady of the house would have to do her own cooking and not wanting to put her in the embarrassing position of having to open her own front door, no one who was aware of the situation made calls on Sunday afternoons.

Children, too, soon learned that Chinese servants had minds of their own. A man who had been in the employ of Nellie Gillespie's father was rehired at a lower rate of pay. After a while Nellie asked him, "Why don't you make those nice jelly tarts you used to make?''

"Oh, $20 Chinaman not make tarts like that. $25 Chinaman make them,'' he replied.[27]

Ada McGeer, born on Niagara Street in 1890, enjoyed a special relationship with Joe, the family's cook. Joe became very irritated when she dawdled on her way home for lunch. Finally he laid down the law. When the meal was ready, Joe said, he would blow a horn and if Ada didn't arrive promptly she would get no lunch. "He would wait until I crossed the road in front of the house,'' Ada fondly recalled, "and then he would make a great to-do with the horn.''[28]

Children could become the bane of Chinese lives. On his way into town Gee had to pass a piece of vacant land on which neighbourhood boys had established their headquarters. "One day they knocked him off the sidewalk, and at the same time cut his head so badly with a stone that he rushed home to me, and I had to plaster and bandage his head and eye,'' Florence recalled.

When she phoned the police to report the incident, she was told, "Well, I guess if he is scared he best stop at home, or you could walk down the street with him, they won't go for him if you are there; we are too busy to look after every Chinaman that has a stone thrown at him.''

"I'm afraid some of the boys used to chase them and pull the pigtail,'' an elderly Chief Justice remembered, adding hopefully, "but I don't think I ever did it myself.''[29]

While some Victorians regarded the Chinese as objects of sport, others found them fascinating. Chartres Pemberton watched with growing admiration as the Chinese market gardners cleared the forest west of Moss Street.

HOUSEBOY, *at Robert Rithet's home 'Hollybank'.*

"They first cut deep trenches around the bases of the trunks, severing the enormous roots at about ten feet from the trunks," he wrote. "The trees were then left standing. The first winter gale overturned the trees, and in doing so pulled up the stumps."[30]

The Chinese brought an exotic quality of life to Victoria. Crowds gathered as funeral processions, with their complement of richly costumed, flag-carrying mourners, wound through town. And during Chinese New Year, residents were drawn to Chinatown which was loud with fire-crackers and bedecked with banners and huge paper lanterns. As part of the festivities Chinese merchants extended a special welcome to their customers. "They'd give you the most wonderful reception there — they'd give you the best to be had in the way of drinks and cigars and generally a little present."[31]

Wealthy Victorians owed a great deal to the small army of Chinese servants who cooked the meals, cleaned the houses, maintained the lawns and gardens and allowed them to enjoy a life of genteel leisure. And when Benjamin Pearse wrote his will he may have felt that he was acknowledging that debt when he bequeathed fifty dollars of his $200,000 estate to his houseboy, Hing.

6.
"tea and strawberries"

To have been young and beautiful and a member of one of the city's first families during Victoria's heyday must have been something approaching bliss. For Kathleen O'Reilly life at 'Point Ellice' came so close to perfection that she could never bring herself to leave her home for more than a few months. (*site 55*) She was born at 'Point Ellice' and, except for the years during which she attended a London finishing school, she spent her childhood there. In 1891 she was twenty-three, an adored, only daughter graced with a beauty that was timeless rather than simply fashionable. For her, life in Victoria was particularly golden.

Summer was a blur of social events; dinner parties at 'Ashnola'; garden parties at the 'Laurels'; picnics at the Tyrwhitt-Drakes; boating parties along the Gorge; crabbing parties at Cordova Bay to which Kathleen rode across the countryside on her horse Blackie; dances at Government House, 'Mount Adelaide' and 'Highwood' which often went on till three or four and from which Kathleen strolled home through morning streets if her carriage had not arrived to collect her; riding parties with the Pembertons; and tennis parties at Sir Matthew Baillie Begbie's.[32]

Begbie's enthusiasm for the game had helped make tennis one of the most popular summer diversions. The O'Reillys had only one tennis court and limited their guest list to twenty-five or thirty. Begbie, with three of the best courts in town, entertained at large bi-weekly parties and became a discriminating critic of the parties given by others.[33]

CHARLOTTE KATHLEEN
O'REILLY.

He reluctantly admitted that he couldn't compete with one hostess who had a "good cow" and provided her guests with ice-cream, which Begbie grumbled, "I cannot for love or money get any confectioner to make." But at least he could take pride in the superiority of his courts to the one at Highwood. (*site 45*)

"Mrs. Ward tried to have them [tennis parties] but you know her ground; though everybody likes her immensely nobody cares, even to oblige her, to play on it, so bumpy and uncertain . . ," Begbie wrote, taking more pleasure than pain from Mrs. Ward's social problems.

During the winter and on those few summer days when they had not received invitations, Kathleen and her mother drove about in their carriage calling on friends and family and leaving their cards if no one were home. When they returned to 'Point Ellice', they rushed to the hall table to examine the cards left by the ladies who had called on them. Often they would discover that a party of naval officers, who had stopped by to visit Peter O'Reilly, had been invited to stay for lunch or tea or dinner and were happily making themselves at home.

At least one naval officer wooed, and for a time thought he had won, Kathleen. Lieutenant-Commander Henry Scudamore Stanhope, the thirty-six year old heir to the Earl of Chesterfield, was a frequent guest at 'Point Ellice' during the summer of 1891 — invited to tennis parties or for dinner and dropping by for tea and strawberries.

The day before a promotion required him to return to England, Stanhope, who had been given every encouragement to believe he would be accepted, proposed to Kathleen. Kathleen did not say yes, but she admitted, "I did not say no." When Stanhope suggested he speak to her father, Kathleen demurred. Her affection for him "frightened" her, Kathleen hedged. It had all been so sudden. She needed time. Would he wait for her answer, she asked, hinting that he wouldn't have to wait long but intending to unpick the web in which she found herself tangled once he was safely in England. To her father she confided the truth.

SIR MATTHEW BAILLIE BEGBIE, *on one of the tennis courts at his Fairfield house.*

"I did not want to be married. I love being here with you all."[34]

Although her family possessed only a fraction of their wealth, Kathleen clearly felt herself superior to the Dunsmuirs. Invited to serve as one of Jessie Dunsmuir's bridesmaids at her wedding to Sir Richard Musgrave, Kathleen declined, flitting over to Vancouver to attend a performance by Sarah Bernhardt instead.

Secure in her position in society and fully appreciating the charm of the life she led, Kathleen dallied too long. She remained at 'Point Ellice' through two world wars; she saw the Gorge begin to decline as industry slipped in and as large estates were divided and sub-divided into smaller and smaller holdings. She died, a spinster, at 'Point Ellice' in her seventy-eighth year.

Other than the complications of love affairs and the social gaffes of holding tennis parties on an inadequate court or staging a ball on a hot August evening with perspiring guests dancing little and leaving early, life seems to have held few terrors for Kathleen and the members of her set. Even a smallpox epidemic could result in unexpected pleasures rather than panic.

On April 17, 1892 the *Empress of Japan* sailed into Victoria with a yellow flag flying, indicating that smallpox was on board. Only one Chinese was found suffering from the disease but all the Chinese passengers were put through quarantine at Esquimalt. That seemed precaution enough and white passengers were allowed to disembark. By summer smallpox had become epidemic in Victoria. (*site 33*)

"We were really, really frightened," Nellie Gillespie recalled.[35] As smallpox spread through the town, yellow flags were hung in the windows of affected houses. At first attempts had been made to move all victims to the quarantine hospital, but the hospital was old and dirty and, as one sufferer remembered, " . . . they didn't have any nurses that would undertake to go there."[36] A separate building at the Royal Jubilee Hospital was prepared but the notion of confining a member of one's family to the hospital or to

131

the camp that was established ominously close to Ross Bay Cemetery met with resistance.

There was a large family on Johnson Street, Nellie remembered. "One of the children had smallpox and the doctor came and I think an ambulance. They tried to move the girl to the hospital for quarantine and the father wouldn't let her go. He stood on the street with a gun and he said he'd shoot the first man that stepped over his door . . . he wouldn't let her go to the quarantine. I think he thought it was signing her death warrant to have done it."

As the number of cases increased, most victims were cared for in their homes. With more and more yellow flags appearing, some Victorians decamped to hotels in Vancouver and Seattle where they sat out the epidemic.

Florence Baillie-Grohman was forced to consider other alternatives. That summer her husband was away, tramping around the Kootenays trying to get his canal building scheme organized and Florence was alone in Victoria with two small children. When yellow flags appeared in the houses on either side of her, the doctor advised her to leave. Borrowing camping equipment, Florence established herself near the Esquimalt Lagoon where she lived under canvas with her children and their English nursemaid, and her Chinese servants.

So idyllic was Florence's encampment that she was joined by two Pemberton girls and their friend Kitty Beavan, the mayor's daughter. With all social events in the city cancelled, they spent three happy months, taking a daily dip in the sea and singing around evening campfires while Kitty played the banjo, their week-ends enlivened by visits from the Pemberton and Beaven boys, who came from town with news and supplies.

TENNIS PARTY, 'Point Ellice.' Three naval officers are sitting with Kathleen. Peter and Caroline O'Reilly are seated on the bench beside the steps. Wearing a pith helmet is Rear-Admiral, Sir Michael Culme-Seymour.

7.
"the Queen's Birthday"

Signs of an impending smallpox epidemic had not dampened the enthusiasm with which Victorians celebrated Queen Victoria's May 24th birthday. In the early days, the day had been spent cheering on the combatants at the Beacon Hill Park race course. By 1870 the navy was taking an active role in the festivities. "The excitement equalled a Derby Day," Lieutenant Eardley Wilmot of the *Zealous* reported, one horse race between marines and sailors being decided only after "a good deal of hard swearing."[37] That evening the band of the *Zealous* played till dawn at a Government House ball and the following day a naval regatta was held with the costumed sailors using shovels for oars churning around Esquimalt harbour.

By the 1890's the holiday had expanded into a celebration lasting three or four days and the festivities had become centered on the Gorge. "There were people in the thousands . . . everything they could possibly float was up there that day." Indians from the Queen Charlottes arrived with their huge dug-out canoes. Robert Rithet's smart little launch *Hollybank* chugged up and down the Gorge taking his guests to the best vantage points. The single sculls of the James Bay Athletic Association dodged the rowboats of less experienced oarsmen. "It was packed and jammed — a tremendous show."[38]

The show, everyone agreed, depended on the Navy. The route from Esquimalt to the Gorge was lined with pubs and the seamen, most full-bearded

MAY 24TH REGATTA, GORGE. Launches and longboats, canoes and rowboats — everything that could float carried thousands up the Gorge to witness the races.

and all wearing their summer-issue of wide-brimmed straw hats with ribbons bearing the name of their ship encircling the crown, stopped at each one on the way.

"They'd get gloriously drunk," one masculine admirer recalled.

After the more serious races were concluded, the real fun begán — novelty races, such as the one in which the competitors set out at the sound of a gun and when a second gun fired, hurled themselves into the water and then clambered back aboard to continue the race; and the highlight of the afternoon, the greasy pole event.

A heavily greased boom was swung out from the man-of-war which had carried the officers to the party and which was anchored at the mouth of the Gorge. At the end of the boom was a box containing a pig, loud with anticipatory squeals. The object of the game was to run along the pole and pull a string which released the pig sending it splashing into the water. Competitors then dived into the water to retrieve it.

The event was usually won by a sailor, wearing his uniform, or a pirate costume, or something less. "Some of them took their tops off and some had their britches, and their britches would come down before they started to run," an onlooker recalled.

"Of course the whole bank was covered with women and girls and everybody and they'd see these sailors go gliding out there with no . . . ," he paused, discretion preventing him from continuing.[39]

PICNIC PARTY, GORGE. *On May 24th or any other summer weekend, elaborate picnics were a popular form of entertaining.*

The Queen's Birthday celebrations in 1896 promised to be even more spectacular. In addition to the Gorge regatta, the climax of the four day holiday was to be a military tattoo and a sham battle, staged at Macauley Point on Tuesday, May 26.

With crowds of people anxious to get to Macauley Point, all available street-cars were pressed into service on the Esquimalt run and, because it was a special occasion, conductors ignored the fact that their cars were loaded above normal capacity.

At about twenty minutes to two that Tuesday afternoon, Car 6, one of the company's older, smaller, lighter cars left town for the Point Ellice Bridge followed by Car 16, newer, larger and carrying more than 140 passengers. As they neared the bridge, Car 16 slowed to allow the first car to reach the end of the span and a woman tourist from Seattle took advantage of the lull to ask the conductor to open her window, an insignificant act that probably saved her life.

Once the first car had gained the opposite bank, Car 16 rolled forward. After it had travelled thirty or forty feet, there was an odd cracking sound and Car 16 dropped a foot and a half. It continued to move forward for a second or two and then the air was split by a second loud crack and the street-car and the collapsing center span of the bridge plunged down into the water below.

Pleasure boaters, who had been spending a lazy afternoon idling along the Gorge, were jolted into action and paddled furiously for the submerged car while water-side residents scrambled down the bank to the nearest boathouse. Soon a small armada had converged below the bridge's broken span. Exhibiting heroism, or at least presence of mind, the Tyrwhitt-Drake girls managed to pull seven choking people from the water. As the *Colonist* would note approvingly, "class distinctions were forgotten."

Too soon only lifeless bodies were being hauled out of the water to be laid side-by-side on well-groomed lawns. Women from Gorge-side houses tore curtains from their windows to serve as blankets and shrouds and rushed to and fro with brandy, trying to comfort survivors who stumbled about among the corpses looking for the child, the husband or wife, the brother or sister or friend who had been beside them when the bridge collapsed.

The final death count was appalling. Fifty-five men, women and children were dead — crushed by the falling bridge timbers or trapped in the street-car and drowned. Before Victorians fully appreciated the enormity of the disaster, or began to ask awkward questions about its cause, odd stories, the quirks of fate that had saved some and doomed others, began to emerge.

Three horse drawn carriages had been setting out across the bridge at the same time as Car 16. Two had proceeded and had been thrown into the water. Both drivers survived, but the horses trapped in their harnesses had drowned. The third driver had been spared the ordeal when his horse, suddenly and for no apparent reason, reared in its traces and wheeled about carrying him to safety.

"The most extraordinary things happened," a survivor remembered.[40] "People inside were shot out — nobody knows how — out of broken windows."

"My friend . . . the beam hit him on the back of the head and took his head off nearly. Oh, there was a lot of young girls in the front . . . when the bridge came down with all the iron work on top, these girls were caught in there, and they had to take blowtorches the next day and cut the wires out to get those two girls out of that mixture. Terrible thing!" The girls, he shuddered, had only been a few feet from him.

The investigation that followed showed that while fate had selected individual survivors, the accident itself had been caused by negligence. The bridge had been built in 1885, five years before the first street-car had cross-ed it. It was designed to support the load of ten tons and the estimated weight of the overloaded street-car had been more than twice that amount. Fur-thermore the bridge had shown signs of weakness three years earlier, sagg-ing a full three feet when the same Car 16, that had carried fifty-five people to their deaths, had ventured across. Bore holes drilled at the time to inspect the wooden beams had not been filled and the water that collected in them was suspected of having contributed to the rot which led to the ultimate col-lapse. And finally the man charged with inspecting the bridge had accomplish-ed that task less than a month before the disaster simply by rowing under it and then walking over it and noting the vibrations caused by passing traffic.

CAR 16, POINT ELLICE BRIDGE. *This photograph was taken after a small flotilla of pleasure boats had carried the victims from the scene and after Car 16 had been hauled out of the water and onto the beach.*

In the end the City and the street railway company were found to be equally liable and Victorians found their city described with a new unlooked-for superlative.[41] It was the scene of the worst street-car accident ever to occur in North America.

VI. The Great War

1.
"gall and wormwood"

The federal census of 1891 provided more than a hint of what the future would hold for Victoria. When the last census had been taken ten years earlier, Vancouver had not existed. Now its population was 13,709, only three thousand less than that of Victoria. Members of the city council, who had confidently predicted that the census would show that Victoria housed 25,000 residents, demanded a recount. And when the federal authorities insisted that their results were accurate, the city hired its own census takers who were expected to find the nine thousand Victorians who had somehow eluded the federal enumerators. The twenty-six men sent to accomplish this task reported that nearly everyone they visited was indignant at the federal results and was "very willing to do his or her part towards rectifying a serious blunder." With that kind of cooperation it was hardly surprising that they were able to report a final count of 22,981. The result was "gall and wormwood" to Vancouver, the *Colonist* crowed.[1]

While neither city was prepared to acknowledge the progress of the other, both Vancouver and Victoria continued to grow, benefitting from a continent-wide period of economic expansion. In Victoria the Board of Trade, energized by the mood of optimism, built a four story headquarters on Bastion Street in 1892 (*site 17*) and during the same year the proprietors of the Driard added to the hotel once again, spending $275,000 to build its Broad Street wing, six stories high, accented by gracefully curved bay windows and topped by three towers. (*site 20*)

Construction slowed for a few years when Victoria like other North American cities felt the effect of the depression which struck in 1893, but when the economy improved the city's businessmen were quick to add to the growing stock of imposing commercial buildings. In 1896 Simon Leiser's three story brick warehouse (*site 24*), decorated with finials and a band of terra cotta rosettes, appeared on Yates Street at the corner of Waddington Alley and on Government Street the Bank of Montreal began construction of its Chateau-style Victoria branch. (*site 18*)

During the winter of 1897 - 1898 business in Victoria was given a boost by a second gold rush. On July 17, 1897 the steamer *Portland* sailing out of St. Michael, Alaska docked at Seattle and off-loaded sixty-eight prospectors and two tons of gold and the rush to the Klondike was on. "Ho for the Klondike!" was the cry that rang out as west coast cities leapt joyously into competition, each claiming to be the best jumping-off place for the northern goldfields. Victoria's Board of Trade rushed into production of a pamphlet which pointed out an advantage the city enjoyed over San Francisco and Seattle. Victoria was the gateway to "The quickest route, The nearest route, The safest route, The cheapest route" and most important of all "The Duty Saving Route."

CUSTOM HOUSE, *Wharf Street. During the winter of 1897 - 1898, crowds of Klondike-bound men lined along Wharf Street to buy their miners' licenses at the Custom House.*

The goldfields were in Canada and Canadian law required that each prospector entering the territory bring with him enough supplies to make himself self-sufficient for a year. Prospectors could avoid paying import duties if they purchased their supplies in a Canadian city and soon Victoria's Johnson and Yates Streets became clogged with piles of carefully packed supplies ready to be hauled down to the docks for loading aboard a Klondike-bound steamer.

JOHNSON STREET. *B. Williams, Clothier and Hatter, expanded his store and proclaimed himself to be a Klondike Outfitter.*

"Don't go to the Klondike without an Albion stove," the Albion Iron Works warned and introduced three new portable models. Clothiers W. & J. Wilson proclaimed themselves to be "Klondike Outfitters" and druggist Thomas Shotbolt discovered that his large stock of Vasoline rapidly began to disappear after he advertised it as a cure for frostbite. Victoria's store-keepers supplied Klondikers with everything they needed — sleighs, high boots, buckskin bags, moose hide moccasins, woolen mitts and hats, saddles, shovels and sacks — everything but dogs.

"You'd have to keep your dogs tied up," one resident recalled. "Any sort of a dog — a setter or anything else that could pull a sleigh — they'd get him aboard."[2]

Amid the excitement, as Victorians scrambled to take advantage of the business bonanza, the federal government began construction of a new post office on Government Street beside the Inner Harbour. And while Victorians grumbled about its style, the new building was a statement of confidence in the city's future. Three years later, when the latest census results were released, it seemed as if that confidence might have been misplaced. Victoria's population was 20,816; Vancouver's had mushroomed to 26,133. And it was Victoria's turn to taste the gall and wormwood of being in second place. The city was no longer the largest in the province. Its industrial base was slipping away to the mainland. Victoria would have to explore new economic solutions if it wished to survive.

2.
"Always be proud and glad you're British"

By the turn of the century, two men had begun to work a particular magic on Victoria. Samuel Maclure and Francis Rattenbury shared the profession of architecture, but otherwise it would be difficult to imagine two more different men. One excelled in residential design; the other became the province's foremost corporate and government architect. For one, architecture was an art; to the other it was a business. One died in his own bed surrounded by his family; the other was clubbed to death by his wife's jealous lover. Both left buildings that came to symbolize Victoria.

The son of a Royal Engineer, Sam Maclure was born in New Westminster in 1860. Trained as a telegraph operator, but drawn to artistic pursuits, Maclure spent a year studying at the Spring Garden Art School in Philadelphia. Perhaps inspired by the urban sophistication of Philadelphia and New York as compared to the raw frontier newness of New Westminster, Maclure included architecture-related subjects in his course of studies. Some theoretical knowledge, combined with artistic sensitivity, more than qualified him as an architect at a time when no professional standards had been agreed upon. In 1892, after having established himself as an architect in New Westminster, Maclure moved to Victoria.

By the turn of the century he was well on the way to becoming the city's premier residential architect, for he had solved a design problem that had confounded earlier architects and plagued their clients — and he had done it in a way that was at once *avant garde* and traditional.

Since almost all entertaining was done at home, Victoria's great houses were required to perform two opposing functions. They had to be family homes in which residents could live with some comfort, but at the same time they had to serve as the setting for lavish entertainments — balls, fancy dress parties, receptions — with guest lists of a hundred or more. A home in which one could live without being chilled to the bone during Victoria's windy winters needed relatively small heat-trapping interior spaces and even Victoria's grandest houses were divided into separate single-purpose rooms, entered through narrow doorways and existing in apparent isolation from the rest of the house. Crowded with furniture and cluttered with bric-a-brac and with dark papered walls and heavy draperies, interiors began to feel cramped and stuffy when more than a few people gathered.

MACLURE INTERIOR, *Foul Bay Road.*

Maclure's houses were stripped of fussy architectural embellishment. Ceilings were lowered and plastered walls were bathed in white, accenting wood panelling and reflecting light from generous windows. Rooms on the lower floors opened off large central halls. Within seconds wide sliding doors could be made to disappear and family apartments became spacious and welcoming, ready to receive guests who could mingle, dance or listen to concerts, feeling at home but comfortably uncrowded.

In their shape and their management of interior space, Maclure houses owed more to the "Prairie" houses of Frank Lloyd Wright than to English historical architectural forms and part of Maclure's ingenuity lay in the manner in which he made his designs acceptable to the most tradition-bound clients.

Many of Maclure's clients had been born in Victoria or on Vancouver Island, but if they thought of themselves as Canadians that was only because

Canada was part of the British Empire. Their hearts and loyalties belonged to England. England continued to be "Home."

James Dunsmuir's daughter Byrdie and her husband Guy Audain lived in 'Ellora', a Maclure-designed house on Foul Bay Road. Byrdie was a second generation Vancouver Islander, but she thought of herself as neither British Columbian nor Canadian.

"Always be proud and glad you're British," Byrdie adjured her son, "there is nothing like it in the world."[3]

Nostalgic for an England they had never known or that they had experienced only during their school years, and living in a society still dominated by the officers of the Royal Navy, Victorians were manoeuvered into accepting a progressive architectural form by Maclure's use of traditional decorative touches, particularly by his adaptation of Tudor, the most recognizably English of all building styles, to houses that might have otherwise appeared frankly North American. Interiors were reminiscent of Tudor country houses. Sturdy beams of polished wood warmed starkly white ceilings. Central halls, panelled in oak to the first floor, were heated by fireplaces of baronial simplicity and proportions. Tudor half-timbering, dark brown boards set in creamy stucco, decorated exteriors of Maclure-designed mansions.

'ELLORA', *550 Foul Bay Road. Built in 1911, 'Ellora' was surrounded by a four acre garden which included a tennis court and croquet lawn.*

So popular did Maclure houses become that more than thirty were built in the Rockland area and others appeared in Oak Bay. To drive along Rockland Avenue and out to Oak Bay past a seemingly never-ending series of Tudor mansions, designed by Maclure and by architects who fell into place beside him, left an enduring impression of Englishness. And no one found it odd that the impression had been created by a native-born architect working for native-born clients.

A sensitive and caring man, adored by his family and incapable of making an enemy, Maclure died in 1929 with his wife and daughters at his bedside as he breathed out his last words, "The best is yet to come."[4]

Francis Rattenbury's end would be not nearly so peaceful. He left an embittered, broken family and as many enemies as friends, but like Maclure he left buildings which became identified with Victoria.

Born in Yorkshire in 1867 and having apprenticed with his uncle's architectural firm in Bradford, Rattenbury arrived in British Columbia in 1892. A few months later, he began his Victoria career by pulling off the biggest architectural coup in the province's history. Twenty-five years old, unknown, and with little experience, he entered and won the competition to select the design of the new Parliament Buildings. (*site 1*)

The government's decision to replace the old 'Birdcages' had been welcomed by Victorians. Once the government had spent almost one million dollars for new legislative buildings, the possibility of Victoria losing its status as the capital to some mainland city became remote. And feelings of civic relief mingled with provincial pride when the buildings were officially opened on February 10, 1898.

As the architect of the largest, most expensive, and, to Victorians at least, the most important structure built in the province, Rattenbury enjoyed a secure reputation. His buildings began to appear throughout the province — court houses in Nanaimo, Nelson and Vancouver, bank buildings in Victoria, Nelson and Rossland, hotels in Banff and Lake Louise, and in Victoria, a new Government House after Cary Castle was destroyed by fire in 1899.

But his buildings sited on Victoria's Inner Harbour meant the most to Victorians and to him. Until 1901 the city continued to be divided by James

JAMES BAY BRIDGE. *The new post office, standing on the left at the end of the bridge, was completed in 1898. Effluence from the Pendray soap factory, the white building on the waterfront to the right of the bridge, poured into the water, adding a soapy scum to the mud flats.*

Bay, the tidal mud flat that extended well inland and separated the James Bay neighbourhood and the legislative precinct from the downtown business district. The James Bay Bridge had provided a link between the two parts of town, but by the turn of the century the mud flats had become a civic problem that had little to do with transportation.

"There was no rubbish heap anywhere else," a James Bay resident recalled. "It was dumped into the water — old bottles, tins, cans, stoves, and garbage and every mortal thing was dumped there."[5]

In 1901 the City won voter approval to spend tax dollars to replace the bridge with a causeway which would cut the stinking tidal garbage dump off from the sea and allow it to be filled in. Intent on doing away with a civic nuisance, Victoria's ratepayers gave little thought about the use to which the reclaimed land might be put, presuming that the five acres of oozing mud, thirty to forty feet deep, would support little more than grass and might possibly become a public park. But Rattenbury and the Canadian Pacific Railway recognized the old mud flats as nothing less than the most spectacular building site in the city.[6]

The CPR, which had purchased the Canadian Pacific Navigation Company in 1901, was planning to add modern, fast and elegantly appointed steamers to the run between Victoria, Vancouver and Seattle and it was part of the Company's plans that the destination of Victoria-bound passengers would be a CPR tourist hotel. But the Company's directors chose to appear coyly non-committal, hoping to be wooed by a shower of civic favours before they agreed to build an hotel. Victoria's city fathers, aware that Vancouver was fast becoming the centre of commerce and industry and suspecting that the city's future might come to rely on the new industry of tourism, were almost pathetically eager to be made a CPR town. And when the Company allowed itself to be coaxed into building an hotel — provided of course that it was gifted with the land and given a tax exempt status for fifteen years — civic politicians campaigned so enthusiastically that ratepayers overwhelmingly approved the necessary by-law.

Skeptics predicted that the large hotel sketched by Rattenbury for the Company would sink ingloriously out of sight, down and down through the many layers of mud, but the problem of the hotel's foundation was solved by siting it atop wooden pilings driven down to bedrock. When the hotel, christened the Empress, opened in 1908, it was impossible not to appreciate the scope of Rattenbury's vision. He had pictured not just a Chateau-style hotel but a whole harbourscape, a picturesque waterfront, ringed with impressive structures and dominated by buildings he had designed. Rising imposingly above the causeway, the Empress was the centerpiece, the pivotal point around which the whole grand scheme revolved. The first building seen from a deck of a steamer rounding Laurel Point, it would become etched on a visitor's memory as the building which, above all others, he identified with Victoria. Victoria and the Empress; they became synonymous. (*site 7*)

During the 1920's Rattenbury added the CPR Marine Terminal to an Inner Harbour already impressive with his buildings and he provided the inspiration for the CPR's Crystal Gardens. Sited just behind the Empress, the Crystal, a glass-roofed, indoor, salt-water swimming pool, became not only a tourist attraction but also the city's social center, the scene of dances, dog shows, banquets, flower shows, concerts and afternoon teas.

EMPRESS HOTEL. *Soon after the completion of Rattenbury's center block in 1908, work was begun on the extensive rose gardens which became an important part of the hotel's charm.*

If Maclure's Tudor houses represented Victoria's soul, Rattenbury's buildings — the Parliament Buildings, the Empress, the Marine Terminal and the Crystal — defined its heart. It must have been with intense regret that he sailed out of the Inner Harbour never to return, the scandal of his personal life having rendered him a social pariah.

In 1898 Rattenbury married Florence Nunn, one of the adopted daughters of innkeeper John Howard and his wife Nellie. Short and stocky, with a prominent nose and pale blue "frog-like" eyes, Florrie had seemed an odd choice for a successful, handsome young architect, especially since she brought him neither wealth nor increased social standing. But for the first years of their marriage they seem to have been happy enough, living with their two children in the beach-side house Rattenbury had built in Oak Bay. (*site 60*) By the 1920's, however, Rattenbury and Florrie had ceased to speak to one another, communicating only by messages carried between them by their children.

Rattenbury was fifty-six, trapped in a broken marriage and feeling that his architectural career was over when he met Alma Pakenham in 1923. Thirty years his junior, beautiful, giddy, a gifted pianist and a twice-married modern woman who smoked cigarettes in public, Alma represented his last chance for happiness. Or so he thought. He convinced Florrie to divorce him by launching a campaign of harassment that included turning off the heat and light and moving the furniture out of their home. Florrie finally agreed to release him after he adopted the particularly unsettling tactic of bringing Alma home, entertaining her in the garden or in the parlour.

Free of Florrie, Rattenbury married Alma. He found himself shunned at the Union Club and cold-shouldered on the streets by Victorians who had been appalled by his behavior. He remained in the city until 1930 when he was finally convinced that neither he nor Alma would gain re-admittance to the social set that included the families of the lawyers, politicians and businessmen who had been among his most important clients.

FRANCIS M. RATTENBURY   ALMA RATTENBURY

Alma and Rattenbury left Victoria and travelled to England where they settled in Bournemouth. The difference in their ages began to tell. Rattenbury slipped from maturity into old age, becoming increasingly deaf and depending more and more on whiskey to see him through long retirement days.

In 1934 they hired seventeen year old George Stoner to act as their chauffeur. Within weeks Alma seduced him and installed him in the spare bedroom as her lover-in-residence. On the night of March 24, 1935 Stoner, driven wild by the thought that Rattenbury had discovered their affair and would order him from the house, crept into the living room, found Rattenbury dozing in his chair and clubbed him to death.

Both Alma and Stoner were charged with murder. Their trial, one of the most sensational to be conducted in the Old Bailey in this century, concluded on May 31, 1935. Alma was acquitted; Stoner was sentenced to hang. Four days later Alma, unable to face the prospect of Stoner's execution, committed suicide by stabbing herself through the heart.

3.
"speculation fever"

The concessions granted by Victoria to the CPR were perhaps the most effective of all corporate give-aways in the city's history. The Company's "Princess" line of steamers, providing regular fast service to the mainland and Seattle minimized the problem of the city's island location and delivered passengers to the doorstep of the Empress Hotel, to the heart of the business district. The CPR's "Empress" fleet of sleek white ocean liners linked Victoria with ports across the Pacific. British civil servants from India, Singapore, Borneo, Hong Kong and other outposts were introduced to the city on their way home to England for periodic "long leaves" from their colonial responsibilities. Struck by Victoria's Englishness, impressed by its climate and its parks and gardens, and relaxed by the comfort of the Empress, many decided that the city was a good place in which to invest and to retire.

In 1934, when Agnes Newton Keith married Harry, a young Englishman whom she had met when he was on leave from government service in British North Borneo, she shouldn't have been surprised that he owned a home in Victoria.[7] In 1939 when she and Harry left Borneo on his next leave, it was to Victoria rather than to England that they returned. Six years later it was in Victoria that they recuperated after spending the war as prisoners of the Japanese. And it was in Victoria that Agnes wrote "Three Came Home", the account of her life as a prisoner-of-war, which was later filmed with Claudette Colbert playing Agnes.

The thousands of people brought to the city by the CPR's world-wide publicity campaigns contributed to the outbreak of speculation-fever, which gripped Victoria on the eve of the Great War.

CHIPPEWA, *entering the Inner Harbour. An American vessel owned by the Puget Sound Navigation Company, the* Chippewa, *competed with the CPR on the lucrative Victoria-Seattle run.*

Between 1910 and 1913 almost five hundred new members paid the $100 fee to join the Union Club.[8] Most of them were fresh from England, attracted to the city by the unprecedented real estate boom. As it became flush with its new prosperity, the Club began to think about finding more distinguished premises. After more than twenty-five years of gentlemanly occupation the Douglas Street clubhouse was showing signs of wear and tear and the Club's suggestion book was thick with complaints. In August of 1910 a disgruntled diner wrote, "Suggested that the kitchen be put in a sanitary condition at once. *Maggots* instead of *cockroaches* were served to me this morning with my fish."The following year the book contained the cryptic comment, "Suggested that the Secretary be instructed to supply gum boots and umbrellas to members using the lavatory."

UNION CLUB, *Douglas Street. Standing beside St. Andrew's Presbyterian Church, the old clubhouse, built in 1885 at the corner of Douglas and Courtney Streets, had become run down and rat-infested by 1912.*

Blaming the plague of rats that overran the old clubhouse on its proximity to the stables of the Victoria Transfer Company, the Club searched out a new, less equine location, paying over $60,000 for a lot on Humboldt Street opposite the Empress. Completed in 1912, their new premises, designed by Loring P. Rexford of San Francisco, set club members back more than $400,000 but they considered it money well spent. Except perhaps for one unhappy gentleman who suggested in November, 1913, "That a reward be offered by the Club to anyone giving information as to the whereabouts of any freight lift in B.C. which can make one-tenth of the noise made by the lift installed by the Club."

Gripped by the mood of over-heated optimism, the Hudson's Bay Company decided to move its retail store from the Wharf Street building it had occupied since 1859. Picking a location that they felt would become the center of town, the Company purchased the property at the corner of Douglas and Fisgard occupied by St. John's, the old 'Iron Church' which had been built in England of corrugated and cast iron, taken apart and shipped in pieces to Victoria where it was reassembled in 1860.[9] (*site 30*)

St. John's parishioners benefitted rather more than the Company by its choice of the site. No longer would they have to endure sermons made unintelligible by rain hammering on the church's iron roof and the $150,000 the Company paid for the land allowed the construction of a fine church on Quadra Street. Meanwhile the Company had acquired a piece of property which remained on the edge of the town's retail district as other merchants persistently clung to old locations refusing to be drawn north along Douglas in the HBC's wake.

Others shared the HBC's belief that the business district would spread and lots near the corner of Fort and Cook Streets were finding buyers in spite of their $75,000 asking price and the Scott building appeared well out of town at the corner of Hillside and Douglas.

By 1912 the first of Victoria's cluster lamps were lighting downtown streets and ratepayers were grumbling about their extravagance. Plans were being prepared for the construction of two new theatres, the Royal Theatre on Broughton Street and the Pantages on Government. Also on Government, new buildings were replacing the rubble left by the worst fire in the city's history.

Shortly before midnight on October 26, 1910 a fire had broken out in David Spencer's store on Government Street between Fort Street and Trounce Alley. By 3 o'clock in the morning the entire block bounded by Trounce Alley and Government, Fort and Broad Streets had been destroyed. The Five Sisters block, named after the daughters of James Douglas, the Victoria Book and Stationery Company and Spencer's department store were reduced to piles of charred brick. Across Broad Street, the Driard Hotel survived but sustained heavy smoke damage. It was the final blow to the hostelry which had been relegated to second best after the opening of the Empress and its pro-

DRIARD HOTEL, *Broad Street. A week after the great fire of 1910 destroyed their Government Street premises, the Spencers re-opened their department store in the Driard's lobby.*

prietor was happy to accept the $370,000 the Spencers offered for the property. Within a week of the fire, merchandise delivered from their Vancouver store replaced the banana trees and potted palms in the Driard's lobby.

Throughout the city residential construction was proceeding at a breathtaking pace, as large estates were subdivided into small city-sized lots. In the Rockland area, 'Craigdarroch's' twenty-eight acres, sold to a developer after Joan Dunsmuir's death in 1908, were cut into 144 building lots, each selling for $2,750. Everyone who bought a lot was given a chance to win the castle. In March, 1910 the draw was held and the Cameron family, owners of a lumber company, were announced as the lucky winners.

In Fairfield, open land disappeared as speculators carved up the Douglas Estate. From Fairfield Road to the sea, Cook Street had been a "streak of skunk-cabbage bog" running between two dairy farms.[10] Two-wheeled garbage carts, heavy with old kettles, cook stoves and beds, trundled along Fairfield Road and toppled their load onto the unmade street. After heavy winter rains, Cook Street became a pond, shallow enough to quickly freeze on frosty nights. The feverish development that peaked in 1912 and 1913 swept away the cow-yards, the Chinese market gardens and the skaters' pond. Solid Edwardian houses replaced Trutch's orchard and marched down Cook Street all the way to the sea. As Fairfield filled with houses, speculators turned their attention to Oak Bay. Until 1912 Oak Bay had only a few permanent residents. Sam Maclure and Frank Rattenbury both built homes on the waterfront, but to most Victorians Oak Bay remained a summer resort, a place where one could escape the heat and dust and noise of the city to spend the summer months in little beach-side cottages or wooden-floored tents. But by 1912 streets were being cut through farmer's fields, Oliver Street was being advertised as the "Linden Avenue of Oak Bay" and developers were asking as much as $5000 for houses along Monterey Avenue.

By 1914 the speculative balloon, so overinflated that it could do nothing else, burst with a rush that swept away savings and fortunes. Many of the houses in Oak Bay and Fairfield stood empty. The HBC halted construction of its new department store. The Union Club received so few applications for membership that in 1916 entrance fees were temporarily abolished. But the Club's real problem was not the lack of new members but the departure of the old, as men left in droves to take part in the Great War.

4.
"the wildest night"

Victorians greeted the outbreak of war with a burst of heartfelt patriotism. The city's grand homes became the setting for garden fetes during which guests sipped tea in bowers bedecked with the Union Jack — an afternoon's pleasure made all the more sweet by the knowledge that the money raised would support the Empire.

The Willows Fairground was converted into a military installation where volunteers from throughout the province were collected to be trained before being shipped overseas. While the men of the Canadian Mounted Regiment perfected their equestrian skills, foot soldiers practiced trench digging at the Willows and in Esquimalt. Victoria soon became a garrison-town, filled with uniforms and alive with military bands and parades.

One of the first volunteers was Jim Dunsmuir, James Dunsmuir's second son. In August, 1914 within days of war having been declared, Jim joined the B.C. Horse and spent the next few months at the Willows with 632 officers and men and four hundred horses, winning his lieutenancy and the "respect and esteem of his fellow officers and those in his charge."[11]

His sister Kathleen, twenty-two years old when the war broke out, contented herself for a time performing at benefit concerts. But by the spring of 1915 she was in France, working from five in the morning until seven at night, running a canteen, equipped at her own expense, providing soup and mugs of tea to Canadian and British troops disembarking at Havre.

The war was brought home to Victorians in a very real way on March 2, 1915 when the *Colonist* reported that Lieutenant Herbert Boggs, whose father Beaumont Boggs was one of the principals of the Oak Bay Improvements Association, had become the first Victorian killed in action. The following month word reached Victoria that J. Herrick MacGregor, who had resigned as president of the Union Club when he enlisted in the 50th Gordon Highlanders, had been shot down as he "strolled along with a cane under his arm, seemingly unaware that a war was being fought around him."

When the news of the *Lusitania's* sinking reached the city, anti-German sentiment heated Victoria to a boiling point. Thirteen Victorians had met their deaths and one of them was twenty-one year old Jim Dunsmuir. Jim had been impatient to get to the front. The Canadian Mounted Regiment had spent months at the Willows. Returning to their barracks after having escorted other troops as they marched through the city to board the "Princess" boats to begin their journey to France, the C.M.R.s had earned the nickname "See Em Offs". Jim had received permission to resign his commission so that he could join an English cavalry regiment and it was presumed that national pride had encouraged him to book passage aboard the *Lusitania*, a British ship, rather than a still neutral American vessel.

On the night of Saturday, May 8, 1915 the day after the sinking, rumours began to spread through Victoria's bars and saloons that some local Ger-

THE DAILY COLONIST, *May 8, 1915.*

mans had celebrated the *Lusitania's* sinking as a German victory. And so began "the wildest night in Victoria's history." A small group of soldiers, drinking the night away singing patriotic songs in the bar of the Kaiserhof Hotel, decided to climb the hotel's fire escape to the roof where they strung Union Jacks from the flagstaff. Soldiers and civilians gathered to watch and to roar their approval and when someone shouted, "To the German Club," a crowd of three hundred, shouting and singing, marched on the club's Government Street premises. They rushed up the stairs and soon furniture and paintings were sent hurtling through the windows. Chanting "Back to the Kaiserhof!" the mob, which by now numbered five hundred, followed by two or three thousand spectators, paraded back to the hotel. When they had finished, the Kaiserhof was a shambles. "All the plate glass windows on the ground floor were completely smashed; the heavy leaded lights swept away . . . The bar fixtures and contents were smashed to atoms and thrown into the street below or tumbled down the stairways," the *Colonist* reported the following day.

The rioters, by now in a frenzy, moved through town ransacking the businesses of anyone who was German or had a German sounding name. On lower Yates Street, Simon Leiser's warehouse was torn apart; "sugar, flour and fifty pound bags of currants were thrown into the street." Across the street where another Leiser operated a clothing store, socks, shirts and bolts of cloth landed on the sidewalk. "One man came up to me and said, 'What size shirts do you take,' and pushed half a dozen toward me," an onlooker recalled.[12]

Peace was restored at midnight when mounted soldiers arrived from the Willows to bolster the outnumbered police force, but for a few days it was an uneasy peace. The Mayor asked all residents to remain in their homes at night "until the popular excitement has abated." Families of German descent posted guards outside their homes. And a military guard was posted at the Lieutenant-Governor's residence. On the night of the riot a story cir-

THE DUG-OUT, *Corner of Government and Fort Streets.*

culated that the Kaiser had been toasted at a dinner at Government House. The loyalties of the Lieutenant-Governor, Francis S. Barnard, who had begun the omnibus service and later taken over the tramway company, were not suspected. But his wife was Martha Loewen, whose father, a partner in the Loewen and Erb brewery, was German-born and that was enough to call Martha's patriotism into question.

By 1917, when Raymond Chandler arrived in Victoria, the city's war had cooled to grim determination. Invalided soldiers sold Victory Bonds from the "Dug-out" at the corner of Government and Fort Streets and throughout the city parks had been divided into small plots on which families impoverished by the war grew vegetables.

RAYMOND CHANDLER, *1917.*
*Chandler travelled to Victoria to enlist
in the Gordon Highlanders.*

Chandler, who would in the years following the war become famous as the creator of hard-boiled detective Philip Marlowe, was born in Chicago. After his parents divorced, he was taken to England by his Irish-born mother. There he attended Dulwich College Preparatory School, passed civil service examinations and began working for the Admiralty. By 1913 he had returned to the United States. Settling in Los Angeles, Chandler, with an "English accent you could cut with a baseball bat," did not feel at home, but when the war began the following year his American side allowed him to remain neutral. In 1917 when the United States entered the war, he decided that he would only feel comfortable in a British uniform and he left southern California for Victoria to enlist in the Gordon Highlanders.[13] He was not impressed with Victoria. He found it "dullish, as an English town would be on a Sunday, everything shut up, churchy atmosphere and so on."

5.
"a little bit of Old England"

Chandler's characterization of the city remained apt for many years. "Nothing at all interesting happened in Victoria after the war," an elderly lady mourned.[14] "Help was impossible to get. Prices went sky high. Everything changed, you know. Nothing was ever the same again." The Camerons lost 'Craigdarroch' to the bank and the castle became a military convalescent hospital. Calling-cards carried in little silver cases became a quaint memory and suddenly it became quite acceptable to dine out at the Empress in something more casual than evening dress. Eggs, at ninety-five cents a dozen, and butter, at seventy cents a pound, became luxuries. And after the passage of an act excluding Chinese immigration in 1923, advertisements for domestics offering twenty-five dollars a month went unanswered.

Vancouver's dominance had become a fact of life with which Victorians would have to learn to cope. After the war, the city found itself overbuilt, years of slow, steady growth being necessary before vacant buildings found tenants and delayed construction projects were completed. Businessmen realized that if they wanted more for their city than years of slow, genteel decay, they would have to aggressively promote its assets.

Enter: the Publicity Bureau and its commissioner, George Warren.[15] Warren and the bureau were determined to make the city attractive to American tourists. Warren toyed with the idea of a recognizable slogan that could be used to categorize the city. In 1918 he coined the phrase "Follow the Birds to Victoria," — a slogan that was used for years, in spite of the fact that anyone arriving in Victoria aboard a CPR steamer couldn't help but notice that the birds had followed them.

After having given the question considerable thought, Warren presented his conclusion to the Kiwanis Club in 1927. "Cities need personality," he said. Victoria could no longer describe itself simply as a "tourist and health resort." What was needed was a slogan or catch-phrase along the lines of the "Outpost of Empire" pioneered in a Tourist Association brochure in 1904.

What was it that set Victoria apart? he asked rhetorically. Well, clearly, the city was a "little bit of old England." And it was to quibble to suggest, as some did, that Victoria was also "a little bit of Japan, China and Hindustan."[16]

Population figures showed that Warren was on firm ground. For thirty years after 1920, more than eighty percent of residents listed their origin as British. And over the years, visitors had invariably mentioned Victoria's Englishness. But something that escaped Warren was the fact that by Englishness most writers were referring not to the appearance of the town, but to its mood or pace and to the tendency of its residents to take the time to appreciate the quality of life the city offered. Earlier tourist promoters, understanding this interpretation, had concentrated on Victoria's beautiful homes, its parks and gardens and had stressed the idea that any city in which it was so pleasant to live must also be a pleasure to visit.

Warren's aggressive promotions, hinged on the "old England" theme, tended to encourage the concept of the city as stage-set. Handsome buildings, such as the Windsor Hotel, were overlaid with a veneer of pseudo-Tudor half-timbering. Thatched cottages appeared where none had existed before. Warren campaigned to have gasoline sold as "petrol" and was almost prostrated when he learned that Victoria's policemen would shed their "English Bobby" helmets in favour of something more American.

The idea of fantasizing Victoria's Englishness wasn't necessarily wrong. Countless tourists have been charmed by the city's interpretation of England's past. But it was unfortunate that in creating the image, too many Victorians neglected the reality. James Douglas' residence, the most historically important house in British Columbia, is gone. 'Cloverdale', the first stone residence in the province was demolished to make way for an apartment building. 'Fernwood' is gone and so are 'Gonzales', 'Armadale,' 'Ashnola', 'Pentrelew' and 'Gisburn'. John Tod's Oak Bay farmhouse, the oldest residence in Western Canada, narrowly escaped demolition, as did 'Craigdarroch', 'Point Ellice', 'Craigflower' and other houses which represent Victoria's real, rather than imagined, past.

Did anyone stop to think that George Warren, the man most responsible for Victoria's belief that it somehow really *was* like old England, was born in San Francisco and had never ventured off the American continent when he began to insist that Victoria was so recognizably English?

Historic Points-of-Interest

The following list provides the locations of sixty-one of Victoria's most interesting historic points-of-interest, many of which are referred to in the text (page references). Sites 1 through 32 are shown on Map 1; 33 through 57 on Map 2. (Please respect the privacy of residents.)

1. PARLIAMENT BUILDINGS. Completed in 1898 at a cost of just under a million dollars, the Parliament Buildings "anchored" the provincial capital in Victoria. (*p. 143*)

2. CHERRY TREE SQUARE. In a tiny square behind the Provincial Archives building, a plaque marks the location of James Douglas' house. (*p.22*) The cherry tree, grown from a slip taken from a tree planted by Douglas, is surrounded by an ornate iron railing rescued when 'Hollybank' was demolished. The square also contains a Coast Forest Garden planted with trillium, evergreen huckleberry, red columbine and a variety of ferns.

3. HELMCKEN HOUSE. Built of squared logs, the oldest part of the house dates from 1853. (*p. 24*) Nearby is the schoolhouse in which the Sisters of St. Ann, an order of nuns recruited in Quebec, began teaching the half-breed children of the HBC's French-Canadian servants in 1858. It has been moved to its present location from site 4.

4. St. ANN'S ACADEMY, Humboldt Street. The cornerstone of the new school and convent was laid in 1871. Three stories high and with its sloping roof broken by five dormers, it can still be seen between later additions. Built in a style common in Quebec, it symbolized the French-Canadian origins of the sisters.

5. CHURCH OF OUR LORD. During the 1870's a doctrinal dispute split the Anglican community. Reverend Edward Cridge, who opposed the "Roman" practices of Christ Church Cathedral, led many parishioners in a revolt against the bishop. The small gothic country church, significantly sited "lower" than the cathedral on the hill, was completed in 1874. Three years later James Douglas, who had donated the land and the organ, was buried from the church.

6. CRYSTAL GARDEN. Designed by Francis Rattenbury and P.L. James, the Crystal was the largest indoor, salt-water swimming pool in Canada. (*p. 144*)

7. EMPRESS HOTEL. Designed by Francis Rattenbury, the Empress was completed in 1908. (*p. 144*)

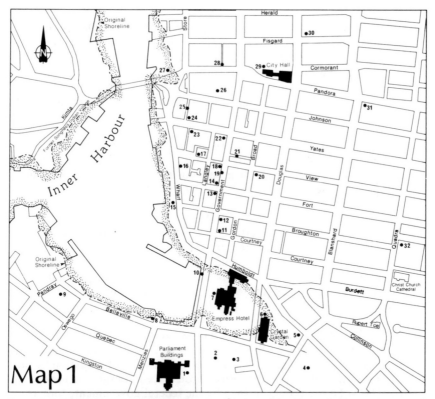

Map 1

8. CPR STEAMSHIP TERMINAL. Designed by Francis Rattenbury and completed in 1924, the CPR Terminal was designed as a temple to Poseidon, the God of the Sea. Poseidon, wearing a crown and supported by crossed tridents, can be seen above the entrance to the building.

9. PENDRAY HOUSE, 309 Belleville Street. Built during the 1890's, the Pendray residence is one of Victoria's finest Queen Anne houses. It became famous for its topiary garden, which included shrubs tortured into the shapes of a beaver and a teddy bear, and for its electrically operated garden fountain.

10. GAS LAMP. The gas lamp near the Visitor Information center is similar to those which began to light the city in 1862. (*p.58*) Early gas meters contained a few drops of water which froze during the winter, cutting off the flow of gas. The gas company decided that the customer should provide the anti-freeze. "The Inspector is instructed to substitute alcohol for the water in the Meters, when furnished with the article by and at the expense of the consumer," a company directive read, "the ordinary kind of whiskey will answer the purpose."

11. WINDSOR HOTEL, 901 Government Street. Completed in 1858, the Windsor was the first brick hotel built in Victoria. (*p. 44*)

12. WEILER BUILDING, 921 Government Street. Built in 1898, the building provided the Weilers with elegantly appointed premises in which to display the furniture they manufactured in their factory at the corner of Broughton and Broad Streets (now the Counting House complex of theatres and restaurants). In 1901, John Weiler's death as the result of an overdose of crude opium suggested that the drug had its devotees outside Chinatown.

13. BANK OF BRITISH COLUMBIA, 1022 Government Street. Originally the premises of the Bank of British Columbia and now housing the Bank of Commerce, the building was constructed in 1886 on the site once occupied by the BACHELORS' HALL. (*p. 12*)

14. SOUTHGATE-LASCELLES BUILDING, 1102 Government Street. Built in 1869 by business partners J.J. Southgate and the Hon. Horace Lascelles (*p. 54*), the structure is one of the oldest commercial buildings in the city. At the rear of the building is an extension built on the site of the fort's bell tower. (*p. 12*) This recent addition to the building, so carefully blended with the old as to be almost indiscernable, is a microwave tower.

15. MOORING RINGS, CUSTOM HOUSE. Imbedded in the rocks below the little park on Wharf Street are mooring rings, the only remnant of Fort Victoria, which stood within the area bounded by Bastion Square and Government, Wharf and Broughton Streets. Beside the park is the CUSTOM HOUSE built in 1875 by the federal government, four years after B.C. entered Confederation. The building's French-mansard style was common in Eastern Canada, but relatively rare in Victoria and was a suitable choice for an Ottawa-based government.

16. RITHET BUILDING, 1117 Wharf Street. During the gold rush, building materials were shipped north from San Francisco. The cast-iron pillars at the north end of the building bear the imprint of their maker "P. Donahue, Union Ironworks, S.F. Cal. 1861." A caduceus, the wand of Hermes, appears at the top of the pillar. Since Hermes was the god of commerce, the caduceus was an appropriate symbol for commercial buildings and perhaps even more appropriate if one considers that Hermes was also the god of cunning, trickery and theft. Inside the lobby of Tourism British Columbia are the remains of an old well discovered when the building was renovated in 1976. (*p. 44*)

17. BASTION SQUARE. In 1971 the city won a Massey Award for "excellence in the urban environment" for Bastion Square, created when Bastion Street was blocked off and filled in. Built in 1889, the SUPREME COURT BUILDING, (now the Maritime Building), was designed by Hermann Otto Tiedemann, architect of the 'Birdcages'. The style of the court house was without local precedent and it was concluded that it was based on a building in the architect's native Germany. In 1901, $4000 was

spent to install the ornate open-cage elevator — the oldest operating elevator in the province. The court house occupies the site of the POLICE BARRACKS which was built in 1859 and served as jail, court house and the first city hall. Public hangings took place in the barracks-yard, the area between the building and the Yates Street parking garage. (*p.46*) THE BOARD OF TRADE building, on the other side of the square was built in 1892, when Victoria was British Columbia's largest city and local optimism was high.

18. NORTH-EAST BASTION. A plaque on the building at the corner of Government Street and the entrance to Bastion Square marks it as the site of Fort Victoria's north-east bastion which was demolished in December, 1860 during the gold rush. The plaque was unveiled in 1928 by Emmeline Jane, the daughter of fur trader John Tod. (*p. 27*) The Bank of Montreal was built in 1896, on the site of Thomas Harris' house, following the plans prepared by Francis Rattenbury, architect of the Parliament Buildings and the Empress Hotel. (*p. 143*)

19. COMMEMORATIVE BRICKS. In the pavement between Munro's Books and E.A. Morris, are the first in a series of bricks which will outline the perimeter of Fort Victoria and commemorate the city's pioneers. The brain-child of former city archivist Ainslie Helmcken, grandson of Dr. J.S. Helmcken (*p. 22*), the first two in place remember Thomas Harris, Victoria's first mayor (*p. 53*) and Emma Staines, schoolmistress at Fort Victoria (*p. 13*) Emma is correctly, but perhaps rather quaintly, identified as Mrs. Robert Staines.

20. DRIARD HOTEL AND VICTORIA OPERA HOUSE. Eaton's department store is housed in the Driard Hotel and the Opera House. Along Douglas Street is the Driard's 1885 addition. The matching facade along View is the theatre. (*p. 109*) Along Broad Street the curving bay windows mark the hotel's 1892 addition. (*p. 138*) Spencer's department store occupied the buildings from 1910 (*p. 149*) until 1948 when the business was acquired by the Canada-wide T. Eaton chain.

21. TROUNCE ALLEY. Although View Street appeared on early plans, it became blocked by buildings during the hectic days of the gold rush. Thomas Trounce, who owned several lots north of the street, opened an alleyway through his property so that he could more easily find tenants for his stores. View Street was not opened from Broad to Government until the fire of 1910 removed the buildings that had been built across it. W. & J. Wilson, at the corner of Government Street and the alley have been doing business on the same site since the 1860's. (*p. 94*)

22. BLANSHARD'S RESIDENCE. A plaque on the federal building marks it as the site of the residence of Richard Blanshard, the first Governor of Vancouver Island. (*p. 17*) The present post office is the third to occupy the site.

23. AMERICAN HOTEL, 533 Yates. Tommy Burnes' brick hotel replaced an earlier wooden version that was destroyed by fire. (*p. 62*) The large doorway which opened on Commercial Alley recalls the days when Victoria's alleys were its busiest commercial streets.

24. LEISER BUILDING, 524 Yates. Built in 1896, the Leiser building was ransacked during the anti-German riots that followed the *Lusitania's* sinking in 1915. (*p. 151*)

25. WADDINGTON ALLEY. Established by Alfred Waddington in 1858, the alley was Victoria's first "planked" street. (*p. 46*) It is the only street in Victoria where wooden paving blocks, a later solution to the problem of muddy streets, can still be seen. At the far end of the alley is Morley's Soda Water Factory, typical of the two and three story brick buildings which began appearing in the city during the 1880's.

26. CIRCLE FOUNTAIN. The fountain at the entrance to Market Square once stood in the roundabout at Hillside and Douglas. The English solution to sorting traffic at busy intersections, the roundabout was found too complicated for visitors unfamiliar with its operation and was replaced with traffic lights. The fountain provides drinking sources for humans, horses and dogs.

27. E. & N. RAILWAY TERMINAL. Built near the site of the original terminal, the new station was opened in 1985 after prolonged civic pressure convinced Via Rail to bring their trains into Victoria once again. (*p. 111*)

28. FAN TAN ALLEY. Named after a gambling game popular in Chinatown, the alley was one of the area's most important commercial streets, open to the public in general during the daytime, but often closed at night. Off the alley narrow passageways lead to inner courtyards. (*p. 124*)

29. CITY HALL. An addition in 1891 doubled the size of the first city hall built in 1878. The dials of the clock, originally lit by gas, are seven and half feet across — a third the size of London's Big Ben.

30. HUDSON'S BAY COMPANY, 1791 Douglas. Construction of the store began during the land boom of 1912-1913 and was not completed until 1920. (*p. 148*) Its Georgian-Revival style is common to HBC stores in other Canadian cities and is something of a Company trademark. A plaque on the building recalls that the site was occupied by the 'Iron Church' described in 1863 as "centrally located in the suburbs."

31. SYNAGOGUE, 1461 Blanshard. Built in 1863 and recently restored, the synagogue is a national historic site — the oldest surviving synagogue in Canada and on the west coast of North America.

32. PIONEER PARK. Charles Ross (*p. 6*) has the unique distinction of having been buried in Victoria's first two cemeteries and having the third named after him. (*site 38*) Ross was buried in the first cemetery, located at the corner of Douglas and Johnson. During the 1860's Ross and other occupants were removed to the new Quadra Street Cemetery, now Pioneer Park. Among those joining Ross are John Work, the Helmcken family and fifty sailors who died while serving on the Esquimalt Station.

33. PEST HOUSE. A stone marker at the base of a small tree in the parkland opposite Beckley Manor, 548 Dallas Road, locates the site of the pest house and the grave of Bertha Witney who died in a smallpox outbreak in 1872.

34. RICHARD CARR HOUSE, 207 Government. Built in 1864 and the birthplace of artist and writer Emily Carr, the house once stood on four acres of property which extended to Beacon Hill Park. (*p. 79, 97*)

35. ALICE CARR SCHOOLHOUSE, 218 St. Andrews. (Private residence) Emily Carr moved into Alice's schoolhouse in 1939 and remained there until her death. (*p. 98*)

36. HOUSE OF ALL SORTS, 646 Simcoe. (Private residence) In the attic of Hill House is a huge spread-winged eagle, painted by Emily Carr on the roof boards during the years she was a landlady. (*p. 98*)

37. CARR BRIDGE, BEACON HILL PARK. Emily's love of Beacon Hill Park prompted Alice to choose it as the site for the monument she erected to her sister. Beacon Hill has been a park since the city's earliest days, appearing as a park reserve in the official city map of 1858. In 1889, Scottish gardner John Blair won the design competition for improvements to the park, and Beacon Hill's lakes and many of its mature ornamental trees date from that time.

38. ROSS BAY CEMETERY. The city's third cemetery Ross Bay was opened in 1872 with the burial of Mary Laetitia Pearse. It is the most historically important cemetery in the province. Within its twenty-seven acres can be found fine examples of Victorian funereal art and it is the resting place of James Douglas, Sir Matthew Baillie Begbie, Amor De Cosmos, Billy Barker, Emily Carr, premiers and lieutenant-governors and one Father of Confederation. In a very real way the cemetery mirrored society. The first families, the Trutchs, the Pembertons, the O'Reillys, and the city's richest families, the Dunsmuirs, the Barnards, the Finlaysons, are buried close to one another in the best section of the cemetery where the view is good and the water table is low. Chinese, buried by number rather than name, indigents like Billy Barker and smallpox victims were buried near the waterfront where the water table is high and where graves were subject to being washed away by winter gales. In a waterfront park above the eastern edge of Ross Bay can be found the Charles Ross memorial

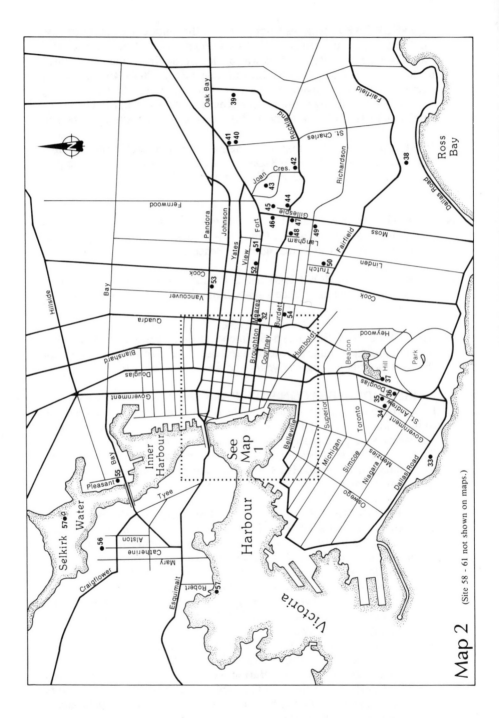

Map 2   (Site 58 - 61 not shown on maps.)

162

bench, erected in his honour in 1967.

39. BIGGERSTAFF WILSON HOUSE, 1770 Rockland Avenue. (Private residence) Completed in 1905, the house was designed by Maclure (*p. 140*) for the son of clothier William Wilson. (*p. 94*)

40. CHARLES FOX TODD HOUSE, 1041 St. Charles Street. (Private residence) Built for the son of Jacob Hunter Todd, the house is one of the best examples of Maclure's Tudor-Revival residences (*p. 140*) and of the upward mobility of those families who made their money "in trade".

41. DAVID HIGGINS HOUSE, 1501 Fort Street. (Open to the public) David Higgins was the editor of the *Colonist*, the author of two books about Victoria's early days, and the president of the street railway company. Built during the 1880's and evidence of Fort Street's fashionable status, 'Regents Park' was rescued from rooming-house neglect by Carl Rudolph who preserved and enriched the building by adding light fixtures, panelling and other bits and pieces salvaged from doomed Victoria mansions.

42 'DUVALS', 1462 Rockland Avenue. (Private residence) Built in 1862, 'Duvals' is one of Rockland Avenue's oldest houses and was for many years the home of the Barnard family, founders of the B.X. and the Victoria Transfer Company. (*p. 115, 152*)

43. CRAIGDARROCH CASTLE, 1050 Joan Crescent. The palatial residence of the Dunsmuirs is open to the public. (*110, 121*)

44. FREDERICK NATION HOUSE, 1320 Rockland Avenue. (Private residence) Built shortly before the war and now converted to apartments, the house added to the impression of Englishness created by Maclure's other Tudor-Revival mansions. (*p. 140*)

45. 'HIGHWOOD', 1021 Gillespie Place. (Private residence) Built during the 1860's, 'Highwood' is perhaps the oldest brick residence surviving in Victoria. Its tennis court and gardens now divided into many residential lots, 'Highwood' can be seen at the end of Gillespie Place presenting its rear facade to the street.

46. LAN DDERWAN, 1040 Moss Street. The Spencers' home (*p. 94*) has been disguised by unsympathetic additions and now houses the Victoria Art Gallery.

47. 'GISBURN' GATES, corner of Rockland and Moss. The gate posts bearing the house's name hint at the spectacular residence to which they served as the entrance. (*p. 120*) Down the block can be seen one of the few hitching posts which remain on Victoria's streets. Another can be found on the 700 block of Linden Avenue.

48. 'LAURELS', 1249 Rockland. (Private residence) The 'Laurels' survived demolition but not modernization. The outline of the house can still be seen, but all its fine decorative details have been obscured by a coat of plaster. (*p. 120*)

49. 1263 Richardson. Robert Ward moved his three-gabled gothic cottage down the hill from Rockland to clear the site for construction of the 'Laurels'.

50. TRUTCH HOUSE, 601 Trutch Street. (Private residence) Built in 1861 for Joseph William Trutch, who became British Columbia's first lieutenant-governor, 'Fairfield' served for a time as the residence of Governor Arthur Kennedy. (*p. 88*)

51. 'WENTWORTH VILLA', 1156 Fort Street. (*p. 77*)

52. 'TREBATHA', 1124 Fort Street. (Private residence) A fine example of residential construction during the 1880's, 'Trebatha' is also an example of misguided modernization. (*p. 111*)

53. HARRIS GREEN. A wide boulevard reminiscent of those found in European cities, the green was named after Victoria's first mayor. (*p. 53*)

54. ANGELA COLLEGE, 923 Burdett. Built in 1865 as an Anglican girls' school, the building is now owned by the Sisters of St. Ann. A fine example of the Gothic-Revival style which became identified with the Church of England, Angela College sits on the street named for its benefactress. Baroness Angela Burdett-Coutts, heiress to a banking for tune, was encouraged by Charles Dickens to become involved in philanthropic works. Although she never visited the Island she became interested in the well-being of the Colony and provided the funds for the 'Iron Church', for Angela College and for the brideship *Tynemouth*. In 1880, when she was sixty-six years old, Angela proposed to William Ashmead Bartlett, her private secretary who was almost forty years her junior. "Lady Burdett really must be crazy," Queen Victoria exclaimed when she heard the news and Bartlett suggested that she adopt him instead. But Angela was adamant. They were married in 1881 and remained together for twenty-five years, until Angela's death at ninety-two.

55. 'POINT ELLICE', 2616 Pleasant Street. For many years the home of the O'Reilly family (*p. 90, 129*) the house remains unchanged and contains the family's original furniture and bric-a-brac. It is now owned by the provincial government and is open to the public.

56. 'ROSLYN', 1135 Catherine Street. (Private residence) 'Roslyn' sits at the foot of Catherine Street and is best viewed from the pathway leading from Bamfield Park. Like other houses sited along the Gorge, it presents its best face to the water.

57. **HALKETT AND COFFIN ISLANDS.** Both Halkett Island in the Gorge and Coffin Island off the foot of Robert Street were Indian burial grounds. The Indian practice of flattening the head led to a brisk trade in oddly shaped skulls during the 1850's. In October, 1856 Annie Deans of Craigflower Farm wrote to friends in England, "You speak of getting some sculls [sic]. I will try and get a Flat Head or two . . . there is a tribe of indians called Neweetes who live on the North end of this Island who has got heads something like a sugar loaf. I would like very well to get one of them." The Indians buried their dead on an island, Annie explained and, "It would be immediate death for a white man to go near it . . . " However, Annie continued, she found some half-breeds who had agreed to become grave-robbers. Their asking price of one dollar per skull was, Dr. Helmcken told Annie, " . . . to [sic] much to give for old bones."

58. **CRAIGFLOWER FARM,** Admirals Road at Craigflower. The only one of the four farms established by the Puget Sound Agricultural Company to have survived, Craigflower is open to the public. (*p. 20*)

59. **NAVAL CEMETERY,** on the south side of the Gorge Vale Golf Course. In 1868 the Admiralty paid $300 for "a turnip field on Constance Cove Farm" and the ground was consecrated as a naval cemetery. Governor Frederick Seymour (p. 71) and the Lieutenant-Commander Lascelles (*p. 53*) were buried here the following year. The wooden markers of ordinary seamen often record the cause of death and the number of eighteen and nineteen year olds who died by drowning or after falling from the rigging suggests the hard lives of nineteenth century sailors.

60. **RATTENBURY RESIDENCE,** 1701 Beach Drive. (Glenlyon School). (*p. 145*)

61. **TOD HOUSE,** 2564 Heron. (Private residence) Built by John Tod in 1851, the house is the oldest residence in Western Canada. It is Victoria's most famous "haunted house." (*p. 27*) During the 1940's Lieutenant-Commander Evans was in residence. A no-nonsense individual, he couldn't help but notice the odd things that happened in the house. Jackets and hats hung on the coat rack in the hall would be found in a tumble on the floor in the morning. The door to the basement would be found open no matter what was propped up against it. And finally Evans was forced to remove from his bedroom the old rocking chair that insisted on rocking at odd times during the night when no one had been near it. A former tenant of the house reported similar experiences. "Sometimes I would wake up in the night feeling a presence in the room. The door would slowly open although I couldn't see a thing," she said. "Sometimes as I was walking along the passage way, I felt that someone was walking beside me . . . It got very tiresome."

I. Fort Victoria
1 Charles Bayley, Early Life on Vancouver Island, (transcript, PABC, c. 1878)
2 Charlotte S.M. Girard, "Sir James Douglas' Mother and Grandmother," *B.C. Studies*, Winter, 1979 - 80.
3 Rev. A.G. Morice, *The History of the Northern Interior of British Columbia, 1660 - 1880* (Toronto: 1904).
4 cited, Derek Pethick, *Victoria: The Fort* (Vancouver: Mitchell Press, 1968)
5 E.A. Collard, *Montreal Yesterdays* (Toronto: Longmans, 1963)
6 *Beaver*, March, 1943.
7 "Five Letters of Charles Ross," *BCHQ*, April, 1943.
8 Roderick Finlayson to James Douglas, June 28, 1844.
9 J.R. Anderson, "Notes and Comments on Early Days and Events," PABC
10 cited, Derek Pethick, *The Fort*.
11 Roderick Finlayson, History of Vancouver Island and the Northwest Coast, typescript, (PABC)
12 J.R. Anderson, "Notes and Comments".
13 *Ibid*.
14 cited, G. Hollis Slater, "Rev. Robert John Staines," *BCHQ*, Oct, 1950
15 Dorothy Blakey Smith (ed.), *The Reminisences of Doctor John Sebastian Helmcken* (Vancouver: U.B.C. Press, 1975).
16 James E. Hendrickson, "Two Letters from Captain Walter Colquhoun Grant," *B.C. Studies*, Summer, 1975.
17 cited, *Ibid*.
18 D.B. Smith, *The Reminiscences*.
19 J.W. Mackay, typescript (PABC).
20 J.E. Hendrickson, "Two Letters from . . . Grant"
21 D.B. Smith, *Reminiscences*
22 cited, Willard Ireland, "Captain Walter Colquhoun Grant: Vancouver Island's First Independent Settler," *BCHQ*, Vol. 17, 1953.
23 cited, *Ibid*.
24 James E. Hendrickson, (ed.), *Journals of the Colonial Legislatures*, Vol. 1 (Victoria: PABC, 1980)
25 cited, W.E. Ireland, "Appointment of Governor Blanshard," *BCHQ*, July, 1944.
26 cited, Peter Cotton, *Vice Regal Mansions of British Columbia* (Vancouver: Elgin Publications, 1981).
27 *Ibid*.
28 cited, D. Pethick, *The Fort*.
29 Bayley, Early Life.
30 "Census of Vancouver Island, 1855," *BCHQ*, Jan, 1940.
31 Anderson, "Notes and Comments".
32 Smith, *Reminiscences*.
33 *Ibid*.
34 Annie Deans, Correspondence Outward, PABC.
35 cited, Sylvia Van Kirk, *"Many Tender Ties"* (Winnipeg: Watson and Dwyer, 1980).
36 George F.G. Stanley (ed.), *Mapping the Frontier, Chrles Wilson's Diary* (Toronto: Macmillan, 1970)
37 cited, Madge Wolfenden, "Notes on the Tod Family," *BCHQ*, July - Oct., 1954.
38 *Ibid*.
39 *Ibid*.
40 cited, Anderson, "Notes and Comments".
41 *Colonist*, January 12, 1861.

[42] cited, Glynn Barratt, *Russian Shadows on the British Northwest Coast of North America, 1810 - 1890* (Vancouver: U.B.C. Press, 1983).

[43] cited, *Ibid*.

[45] "Diary of Martha Cheney Ella," *BCHQ*, July - Oct., 1949.

[46] Captain John T. Walbran, *British Columbia Coast Names, 1592 - 1906* (Vancouver: J.J. Douglas, 1971).

[47] *Colonist*, November 16, 1860.

[48] "Diary of Robert Melrose," *BCHQ*, April, July, October, 1943.

[49] N. Lugrin, *The Pioneer Women of Vancouver Island, 1843 - 1866* (Victoria: 1928) and D.W. Higgins, *The Passing of a Race* (Toronto: Wm. Briggs, 1905).

[50] Lord Charles Beresford, *The Memoirs of Admiral Lord Charles Beresford* (London: Metheun, 1916); Geoffrey Bennett, *Charlie B., A Biography of (Admiral Lord Charles Beresford* [Peter Downay, 1968] Anita Leslie,) The   Marlborough House Set (New York: Doubleday, 1973).

[51] *Colonist*, Sept. 28, 1911.

II. The Gold Rush

[1] cited, D. Pethick, *The Fort*.

[2] Alfred Waddington, *Fraser Mines Vindicated* (Victoria: 1858).

[3] Annie Deans, Correspondence Outward, (PABC).

[4] Waddington, *Fraser Mines*.

[5] Deans, Correspondence.

[6] H.H. Bancroft, *History of British Columbia* (San Francisco: The History Company, 1887).

[7] Matthew Macfie, *Vancouver Island and British Columbia* (London: Longman Green, 1865).

[8] *Colonist*, August 28, 1860.

[9] Waddington, *Judicial Murder* (PABC).

[10] D.B. Smith, *Reminiscences*.

[11] Neville Shanks, *Waddington* (Port Hardy: North Island Gazette, 1975)

[12] *Colonist*, Sept. 8, 1880.

[13] Stanley, *Mapping the Frontier*.

[14] *Colonist*, Nov. 9, 1861.

[15] *Colonist*, Oct. 14, 1861.

[16] *Colonist*, Dec. 24, 1861.

[17] *Colonist*, Dec. 20, 1861.

[18] *Victoria Gazette*, Sept. 20, 1859.

[19] Edgar Fawcett, clipping (n.d., PABC, V.F.)

[20] D.W. Higgins, *The Passing of a Race*.

[21] *Colonist*, Sept. 5, 1862.

[22] *Colonist*, Sept. 24, 1862.

[23] *Colonist*, Oct. 3, 1862.

[24] Cecil Maiden, *Lighted Journey, The Story of the B.C. Electric* (B.C.E., 1948).

[25] Allen Francis, U.S. Consul, Reports to W.E. Seward, Secretary of State.

[26] *Illustrated London News*, Sept. 4, 1858.

[27] Higgins, *Mystic Spring*.

[28] *Ibid*.

[29] Francis, Reports.

[30] *Colonist*, May, 1887.

[31] cited, Crawford Killian, *Go Do Some Great Thing* (Vancouver: Douglas and MacIntyre, 1978).

[32] cited, *Ibid*.

[33] D.B. Smith (ed.), Lady Franklin Visits the Pacific Northwest, (PABC Memoir, Victoria, 1974).

[34] *Victoria Gazette*, August 5, 1858.

[35] *Colonist*, Oct. 11, 1861.

[36] *Colonist*, Sept. 27, 1861.

[37] *Colonist*, Sept. 28, 1861.

[38] Macfie, *Vancouver Island*.

[39] cited, Killian, *Go Do Some Great Thing*.

III. Capital City
1 Francis, Reports.
2 cited, G.V.P. and H.B. Akrigg, *British Columbia Chronicle, 1847 - 1871* (Vancouver: Discovery Press, 1977).
3 Margaret Ormsby, "Frederick Seymour, The Forgotten Governor," *B.C. Studies*, Summer, 1974.
4 Akrigg, B.C. *Chronicle*.
5 cited, Cotton, *Vice Regal Mansions*.
6 Willard Ireland, "The Annexation Petition of 1869," *BCHQ*, Oct., 1940.
7 *Colonist*, Dec. 25, 1881.
8 *Colonist*, 1874.
9 Mifflin Gibbs, *Shadows and Light: An Autobiography* (Washington: 1902).
10 Colonist, May 4, 1872.
11 F.W. Van Reynegom, "Victoria and the Victorians," *The Overland Monthly* (San Francisco: 1875).
12 *Ibid*.

IV. Society
1 Cotton, *Vice Regal Mansions*.
2 cited, *Victoria Historical Review* (Victoria Centennial Celebration Society, 1962).
3 cited, D. Pethick, *James Douglas: Servant of Two Empires* (Vancouver: Mitchell Press, 1969).
4 cited, J.K. Nesbitt, *Colonist*, Sept. 14, 1952.
5 *Ibid*.
6 cited, J.K. Nesbitt, *Colonist*, Aug. 28, 1949.
7 Anderson, "Notes and Comments."
8 Bayley, *Early Life*.
9 Francis, Reports.
10 H.E. Sampson, "Joseph Despard Pemberton," *BCHQ*, April 1944.
11 D.B.Smith, Biographical Appendix, "Bushby Journal, 1858 - 59," *BCHQ*, Jan. 1957 - Oct., 1958.
12 Anderson, "Notes and Comments"
13 *The Northwestern Review*, Seattle, July Aug., 1891.
14 cited, Lugrin, *Pioneer Women*.
15 James Douglas, Confidential Report on Officers, 1863, (PABC)
16 cited, David R. Williams, *"The man for a New Country" Sir Matthew Baillie Begbie* (Sidney: Grays Publishing, 1977).
17 D.B. Smith, Biographical Appendix.
18 *Ibid*.
19 D.B. Smith (ed.), *Lady Franklin*.
20 cited, J.K. Nesbitt, "Old Homes and Families", *Colonist*, June 20, 1954.
21 *Victoria Times*, Oct. 22, 1922.
22 *Golden Jubilee, 1873 - 1923*.
23 *Colonist*, Jan. 15, 1874.
27 J. Stricker, Richard Carr house, A History (Heritage Conservation Branch, n.d.).
28 Maria Tippett, *Emily Carr. A Biography* (Toronto: Oxford University Press, 1979).
29 Ada McGreer, "Agnes Deans Cameron. A Memory," *B.C. Historical News*, Nov. 1974.
30 *Victoria Times*, May 14, 1912.
31 Gwen Hayball, "Agnes Deans Cameron, 1863 - 1912," *B.C. Historical News*, June, 1974.
32 *Colonist*, May 23, 1890.
33 *Colonist*, May 26, 1890.
34 *Ibid*.
35 McGeer, "Agnes Deans Cameron."
36 Judge P. Lampman, Commission on South Park School Drawing Books, Feb. 23, 1906.
37 *Ballarat Courier*, Nov. 2, 1881.
38 Emma McCandlish, Correspondence Inward, PABC.
39 *Ibid*.

V. Victoria's Heyday
1 *Colonist*, Sept. 22, 1880.
2 *Colonist*, March 9, 1926.
3 *Colonist*, July 7, 1889.
4 *Colonist*, Feb.3, 1924.
5 *Colonist*, July 4, 1888.
6 Janet Cauthers (ed.), "A Victorian Tapestry," *Sound Heritage*, Vol. VII, PABC, 1978.
7 Douglas V. Parker, *No Horsecars in Paradise* (Vancouver: Whitecap Books, 1981).
8 *Ibid.*
9 *Ibid.*
10 *Colonist*, April 19, 1895.
11 Parker, *No Horsecars in Paradise*.
12 Cauthers (ed.), "Victorian Tapestry".
13 Parker, *No Horsecars in Paradise*.
14 Chartres Pemberton, Papers, PABC.
15 *Ibid.*
16 "Florence Baillie-Grohman — Her Unpublished Manuscript," *B.C. Historical News*, June, 1968.
17 *Colonist*, March 23, 1872.
18 Chief Bloomfield, Report to Police Committee, April 7, 1886 (VCA)
19 cited, R.E. Wynne, *Reaction to the Chinese in the Pacific Northwest and British Columbia* (New York: Arno Press, 1978).
20 James Morton, *In the Sea of Sterile Mountains* (Vancouver: J.J. Douglas, 1974).
21 *Ibid.*
22 Cauthers, "Victorian Tapestry".
23 cited, Morton, *Sea of Sterile Mountains*.
24 *Ibid.*
25 Florence Baillie-Grohman, *Fifteen Years' Sport and Life . . .* (London: Horace Cox, 1907).
26 *Ibid.*
27 Cauthers, "Victorian Tapestry"
28 Ada McGeer, "Glimpses of Early Victoria."
29 Cauthers, "Victorian Tapestry."
30 C.C. Pemberton, Papers.
31 Cauthers, "Victorian Tapestry."
32 Charlotte Kathleen O'Reilly, Diary, PABC.
33 D.R. Williams, *"The Man for a New Country."*
34 cited, Nesbitt, *Colonist*, Aug. 15, 1971.
35 Cauthers, "Victorian Tapestry."
36 *Ibid.*
37 Lieutenant S. Eardley Wilmot, *Our Journal of the Pacific* (London: Longmans Green, 1873).
38 Cauthers, "Victorian Tapestry."
39 *Ibid.*
40 *Ibid.*
41 Derek Pethick, *British Columbia Disasters* (Langley: Stagecoach Publishing, 1978).

VI. The Great War
1 *Colonist*, Oct. 23, 1891.
2 Cauthers, "Victorian Tapestry."
3 James Audain, *My Borrowed Life* (Sidney: Gray's Publishing, 1962)
4 cited, Janet Bingham, *Samuel Maclure, Architect* (Ganges: Horsdal and Schubart, 1985).
5 Cauthers, "Victorian Tapestry."
6 T. Reksten, *Rattenbury* (Victoria: Sono Nis Press, 1978).
7 Agnes Newton Keith, *Three Came Home* (New York: Atlantic-Little, Brown, 1946).
8 Paul Bissey, *Early and Late Victorians. A History of the Union Club of British Columbia* (Victoria: 1969).
9 Stuart Underhill, *The Iron Church* (Victoria Braemar Books, 1984)
10 Emily Carr, *The Book of Small* (Toronto: Clarke Irwin, 1942).

[11] *Colonist*, May 16, 1915.
[12] Bill Kersey, *Colonist*, Oct. 17, 1976.
[13] Frank MacShane, *The Life of Raymond Chandler* (New York: Penguin Books, 1978).
[14] cited, B. Emery, *Colonist*, August 7, 1977.
[15] Kenneth Lines, A Bit of Old England: the Selling of Tourist Victoria, M.A. Thesis, University of Victoria, 1972.
[16] C.W. Stokes, "Victoria, A Bit of England that is not England," *Canadian Magazine*, August 1919.

Bibliography

Newspapers
Illustrated London News
Victoria (British) Colonist
Victoria Gazette
Victoria Times

Unpublished sources
Anderson, Alexander Caulfield. History of the Northwest Coast. (typescript, 1978, PABC).

Anderson, James R. Victoria in 1850 (typescript, PABC)

_____ . Notes and Comments. (typescript, PABC)

Bayley, Charles. Early Life on Vancouver Island. (typescript, c. 1878, PABC)

Bloomfield, Chief. Report to the Police Committee, April 7, 1886.

Finlayson, Roderick. History of Vancouver Island and the Northwest Coast (typescript, PABC)

Lampman, Judge P. Commission on South Park School Drawing Books, Feb 23, 1906.

Lines, Kenneth. A Bit of Old England: The Selling of Tourist Victoria. (M.A. Thesis, University of Victoria, 1972)

Macdonald, William J. A Pioneer of 1851 (typescript, PABC)

Pemberton, Chartres C. Misc. Papers. PABC.

Striker, Judith. Richard Carr House. A History. (Heritage Conservation Branch, n.d.)

Akrigg, G.V.P. and Helen B. British Columbia Chronicle, 1847 - 1871. Vancouver: Discovery Press, 1977.

Audain, James. My Borrowed Life. Sidney: Gray's Publishing, 1962.

Baillie-Grohman, Florence. "Her Unpublished Manuscript," B.C. Historical News, June, 1968.

_____ . Fifteen years' Sport and Life in the Hunting Grounds of Western Australia and British Columbia. London: Horace Cox, 1907.

Bancroft, Hubert Howe. History of British Columbia. San Francisco: The History Company, 1887.

Barratt, Glynn. Russian Shadow on the British Northwest Coast of North America, 1810 - 1890. Vancouver: U.B.C. Press, 1983.

Bennett, Geoffrey. Charlie B. A Biography of Admiral Lord Charles Beresford. Peter Dawnay, 1968.

Beresford, Lord Charles. The Memoirs of Admiral Lord Charles Beresford. London: Metheun, 1916.

Bingham, Janet. Samuel Maclure, Architect. Ganges, B.C.: Horsdal and Schubart, 1985.

Bissley, Paul L. Early and Late Victorians. A History of the Union Club of British Columbia. Victoria: 1969.

Carr, Emily. The Book of Small. Toronto: Clarke, Irwin, 1942.

Cauthers, Janet. "A Victorian Tapestry. Impressions of Life in Victoria, B.C., 1880 - 1914." Sound Heritage Vol. VII, no. 3. Victoria: PABC, 1978.

Cotton, Peter. Vice Regal Mansions of British Columbia. Vancouver: Elgin Publications Ltd., 1981.

"Diary of Martha Cheney Ella" BCHQ, July — Oct., 1949.

"Diary of Robert Melrose" BCHQ, April — July — Oct., 1943.

Fawcett, Edgar. Some Reminiscences of Old Victoria. Toronto: Wm. Briggs, 1912.

"Five Letter of Charles Ross," *BCHQ*, April, 1943.

Gibbs, Mifflin. *Shadow and Light: An Autobiography*. Washington: 1902.

Girard, Charlotte S. M. "Sir James Douglas' Mother and Grandmother," *B.C. Studies*, Winter, 1979 - 80.

Hayball, Gwen. "Agnes Deans Cameron, 1863 - 1912." *B.C. Historical News*, June, 1974.

Hendrickson, James E. (ed.) *Journals of the Colonial Legislatures of the Colonies of Vancouver Island and British Columbia, 1851 - 1871*. Victoria: PABC, 1981.

Higgins, D.W. *The Passing of a Race*. Toronto: Wm. Briggs, 1904.

_____ . *The Mystic Spring*. Toronto: Wm. Briggs, 1904.

Ireland, Willard E. "Appointment of Governor Blanshard," *BCHQ*, July, 1944.

_____ . "Captain Walter Colquhoun Grant: Vancouver Island's First Independent Settler," *BCHQ*, Vol. 17, 1953.

_____ . The Annexation Petition of 1869," *BCHQ*, Oct., 1904.

Killian, Crawford. *Go Do Some Great Thing*. Vancouver: Douglas and MacIntre, 1978.

Lamb, W.K. "Richard Blanshard," *BCHQ*, Jan. — April, 1950.

Leslie, Anita. *The Marlborough House Set*. New York, 1973.

Lugrin, N. deB. *The Pioneer Women of Vancouver Island*. Victoria: 1928.

McGeer, Ada. "Agnes Deans Cameron. A memory," *B.C. Historical News*, Nov., 1974.

Macfie, Matthew. *Vancouver Island and British Columbia*. London: Longmans Green, 1865.

Melrose, Robert. "Diary." *BCHQ*, July — Oct., 1943.

Morice, Rev. A.G. *The History of the Northern Interior of British Columbia, 1660 - 1880*. Toronto: 1904.

Morton, James. *In the Sea of Sterile Mountains. The Chinese in British Columbia*. Vancouver: J.J. Douglas, 1974.

Ormsby, Margaret. "Frederick Seymour, the Forgotten Governor," *B.C. Studies*, 1974.

Parker, Douglas V. *No Horsecars in Paradise. A History of Street Railways and Public Utilities in Victoria, B.C. before 1897*. Vancouver: Whitecap Books, 1981.

Pethick, Derek. *Victoria: The Fort*. Vancouver: Mitchell Press, 1968.

_____ . *British Columbia Disasters*. Langley, B.C.: Stagecoach Publishing, 1978.

_____ . *James Douglas: Servant of Two Empires*. Vancouver: Mitchell Press, 1969.

Reksten, Terry. *Rattenbury*. Victoria: Sono Nis Press, 1978.

Sampson, H.S. "Joseph Despard Pemberton," *BCHQ*, April, 1944.

Segger, Martin and Douglas Franklin. *Victoria. A Primer for Regional History in Architecture*. New York: American Life foundation, 1979.

Shanks, Neville. *Waddington*. Port Hardy: North Island Gazette, 1975.

Slater, G. Hollis. "Rev. Robert John Staines," *BCHQ*, Oct, 1950.

Smith, Dorothy Blakey (ed.). *The Reminiscences of Doctor John Sebastian Helmcken*. Vancouver: U.B.C. Press, 1975.

_____ . (ed.). *Lady Franklin Visits the Pacific Northwest*. Victoria: PABC Memoir, 1974.

_____ . Biographical Appendix. "Bushby Journal, 1858 - 1859," *BCHQ*, Jan. 1957 — Oct. 1958.

Stanley, George F.G. (ed.). *Mapping the Frontier. Charles Wilson's Diary*. Toronto: Macmillan, 1970.

Tippet, Maria. *Emily Carr: A Biography*. Toronto: Oxford University Press, 1979.

Underhill, Stuart. *The Iron Church*. Victoria: Braemar Books, 1984.

VanKirk, Sylvia. *"Many Tender Ties." Women in the Fur-Trade Society in Western Canada*. Winnipeg: Watson and Dwyer, 1980.

Van Reynegom, F.W. "Victoria and the Victorians," *The Overland Monthly*. San Francisco: 1875.

Waddington, Alfred. *Fraser Mines Vindicated*. Victoria: 1858.

Walbran, Captain John T. *British Columbia Coast Names, 1592 - 1906*. Vancouver: J.J. Douglas, 1971.

Williams, David R. *"The Man for a New Country." Sir Matthew Baillie Begbie*. Sidney, B.C.: Gray's Publishing, 1977.

Wilmot, Lieutenant S. Eardley. *Our Journal of the Pacific*. London: Longmans Green, 1873.

Wynne, Richard Edward. *Reaction to the Chinese in the Pacific Northwest and British Columbia, 1850 - 1910*. New York: Arro Press, 1978.

173

Photographs listed below obtained from the
Provincial Archives of British Columbia:

front cover photo and photos on pages: 4, 13, 15,
26, 27, 29, 32, 36, 42, 47, 48, 49, 54, 55, 62, 64, 70,
72, 75, 77(middle), 78(top), 81, 82, 83, 84, 88, 89,
93, 95(top), 96, 102, 104, 105, 106, 110, 113, 120,
130, 133, 134.

INDEX

Terry Reksten has a marvellous talent for making history come alive. The enthusiasm that she so obviously feels for her subject comes across vividly both in her writing and in the lectures in her popular local history course, "Victoria: A 'Lady' with a Past."

Terry's first book, *Rattenbury* (Sono Nis Press, 1978), a fascinating biography of the architect of many of Victoria's most visible landmarks — the Parliament Buildings, the Empress Hotel, the Crystal Gardens — won the Eaton's Literary Award in 1979. Mrs. Reksten was made an "Honorary Citizen of Victoria" in 1985 in recognition of her writing and her work in heritage conservation.

Terry Reksten lives in Oak Bay, half a block from John Tod's 'haunted' farm house with her husband Don and two daughters, Jane and Norah.